STARTUP

UPSTART

The Evolution of Idea into Company

David D. Cummings

Copyright © 2012 by David D. Cummings
All rights reserved

ISBN 978-1468194562

To Erica, Landon, and Claire

With profound acknowledgments to all of the family members, friends, colleagues, and mentors who helped me get where I am today.

Special thanks to Jennifer Betowt for editing this book, to Mary Betowt for illustrating it, and to my first two companies, Hannon Hill and Pardot, for serving as my inspiration.

up · start

[*n.*, *adj.* uhp′ stahrt; *v.* uhp stahrt′]
—*noun*

1 a person who has risen suddenly from a humble position to one of wealth, power, or consequence.

2 someone who rocks the boat or disturbs the accepted status quo; an upsetter.

3 someone who achieves an unexpected or improbable victory over the favored competitor.

CONTENTS

INTRODUCTION

My decision to write a book on the subject of entrepreneurship stemmed from two distinct yet interrelated impulses. First, I wanted to share some of my own experiences. From my very first venture as a fifteen-year-old with a shareware product designed to help coaches track team statistics, I've found the entrepreneurial journey exhilarating. I've also learned that the personal growth and monetary rewards vastly outweigh the inevitable hardships and headaches that come with business ownership. The bottom line is that I just really enjoy talking about entrepreneurship. I like blogging about it, networking with other entrepreneurs, and sharing stories and lessons learned with other business owners.

But beyond this, I wanted to do something more to actively promote entrepreneurship. Historically, new companies have been the main engine of this nation's economic growth, producing innovative products and services for consumers and accounting for nearly all net job creation. When they start a business, entrepreneurs are doing more than just realizing a personal dream—they're also driving the growth of the economy. All of us have a vested interest in promoting entrepreneurship in every way we can.

In order to do that, we first need to have at least a basic understanding of what it is that we mean by *entrepreneurship*. Unfortunately, the term *entrepreneur* has become so clouded by overuse and misuse that today we're as likely to hear it applied to Michael Jordan as to Bill Gates. But this is a business book, and I'd like to immediately dispense with the mistaken notion that simply acquiring celebrity status or even great wealth makes one an entrepreneur. Oprah Winfrey fits easily into my definition of an entrepreneur—not because she's a highly paid television superstar, but because she has exploited her success for numerous new business ventures into magazine and book publishing, a media production company, and even her own cable network. Oprah has done what I believe all entrepreneurs should do. She has created value in the marketplace by identifying new opportunities in the business world, assembled the resources to take advantage of those opportunities, and opened possibilities to others through her efforts.

My own experience with entrepreneurship has been in the trenches rather than among scholars, policymakers, and economists. But even in the ivory towers of academia and the marble halls of Washington, there's something of a debate over definitions. Some economists confine the definition of entrepreneurship to only those companies who receive external financing. The problem I have with this definition is that it insults the scores of new startups out there—all of those independent technology consulting and home-based businesses—that got off the ground with minimal investments amassed from personal savings, maxed out credit cards, and small loans from friends. The narrow "external financing"-based definition seems to suggest that this sort of small business is not only irrelevant to the economy, but also that self-financing is somehow self-limiting. There's significant evidence to the contrary.

> "My interest in life comes from setting myself huge, apparently unachievable challenges and trying to rise above them...from the perspective of wanting to live life to the full, I felt that I had to attempt it."
>
> — **Sir Richard Branson**

Take the personal success stories of two entrepreneurs who really inspire me: Richard Branson and Michael Dell. Richard Branson epitomizes the notion of an upstart. An avid music fan, he began selling his favorite records out of the trunk of his car in London, later expanding this to a mail order company and a record shop, which by the early 1970s had evolved into the highly successful music label we now know as Virgin Records. Just when the world had branded him a music man, in 1984 Branson brought the rock-and-roll aesthetic to his latest venture—an airline, of all things!—Virgin Atlantic Airways. But Branson didn't stay idle for long. Since then, he has made forays into mobile phones, fitness centers, railways, alternative fuels, and even spaceships.

Coming from someone with no experience in these industries whatsoever, Branson's audacious ventures have consistently raised eyebrows. Time and again, nobody thought he could succeed. But mere decades later, his label is known around the world, people talk on his cellphones every day, his airline continues to compete with well-established legacy carriers, and it looks like Virgin Galactic will be the first entity to bring space travel to the paying public. This is truly the stuff of fantasy. Only an upstart like Branson has the guts and vision to take a crazy chance and make it reality.

While Branson certainly intrigues me, I am perhaps even more inspired by the story of Michael Dell, whose story is even more relevant to my own experience. Dell grew up fascinated by machines and computers and took apart his first personal computer (an Apple II) at the age of 15 to see how it worked. As a high school student selling newspaper subscriptions, he was perceptive enough to target certain demographics who were more likely to buy subscriptions (newlyweds and new arrivals to the area), collecting their names from public records such as mortgage applications and marriage licenses. With his love of computers driving him and a clever sales strategy under his belt, Dell started a fledgling business upgrading computers out of his dorm room at the University of Texas at Austin. Based on his success with this startup, and with just $1,000 in startup capital to his name, Dell acted on a strong hunch that he could build a business by cutting out the traditional middleman and selling new PCs directly to customers. This hadn't really been done before, and while risky, Dell's gamble paid off: Michael Dell enjoyed tremendous success, becoming the youngest Fortune 500 CEO by 1992. More importantly, his vision introduced a whole new way of selling computers that subsequently revolutionized consumer access to computing.

Certain aspects of Dell's story resonate with me on several levels. I also had entrepreneurial ambitions from a young age, when I was always trying to sell something, and I too showed an early aptitude for technology that ended up being my calling. But what I can really identify with is Dell's drive and tenacity. As an undergrad at Duke working around the clock out of my dorm room, I started my first successful company, Hannon Hill, even taking a leave of absence from school to work full-time on the business. Like Dell, I knew that getting my company up and running would require 100% dedication. I couldn't give up, or it would never happen. It was all or nothing. This was no part-time pursuit of a hobby—this was a calling. I think this kind of drive is something that all successful entrepreneurs must have.

Both of these success stories involve entrepreneurs who started from virtually nothing and, on the strength of their good ideas and amazing dedication, were able to build viable companies without seeking venture capital or other outside funding sources. Branson and Dell have served as powerful examples to me in my own path to successful entrepreneurship, not least because I saw that being self-funded was in no way self-limiting. In fact, I'd argue that in their cases, as well as in my own experience, self-funding can be a means to freedom and flexibility. With nobody bankrolling you, you are the master of your own destiny, and you make your own decisions—which, as we have seen in the examples of Branson and Dell, can really pay off. And while Branson and Dell did eventually raise money, they did it on their own terms, after they'd established their companies. The moral of the story? Don't let a lack of venture capital deter you if you've got a strong vision and the tenacity to make it happen.

At the other extreme, some popular definitions of entrepreneurship tend to conflate it with either small business ownership or self-employment. I have no problem with the idea that launching even a very small business is entrepreneurial, but I do have some reservations about saying that self-employment is necessarily so. The best way to illustrate that objection is by sharing the example of two friends of mine, Lisa and Julia. These ladies both have academic credentials, a wealth of experience, and successful track records in business and technical writing. A few years after grad school, Lisa launched her own web-based business. Her staff of fifteen specializes in public relations, web copywriting, and content development. Julia left a position in the Education and Services department of a multinational corporation to form her own LLC, and for the last four years she has been happily freelancing from home.

Lisa and Julia share many of the same interests and talents. In the past they have competed for the same contracts, and at other times they have collaborated on projects. Despite being contemporaries and peers, they don't share the same mindset when it comes to ambitions. Lisa wants to grow her business. She regularly attends meetings of the local chapter of Entrepreneurs' Organization, as well as educational conferences and seminars. She tirelessly seeks to recruit new talent, explore new marketing strategies, and to identify and create new opportunities for her organization. She networks with peers, travels extensively to pitch her company's services, and foresees the day when her own company will be listed on the pages of *Fortune* and *Forbes*. Julia, on the other hand, has no interest in doing any of these things. As she herself will willingly tell you, she doesn't possess what we often call the "entrepreneurial spirit." While self-employment has given her personal freedom and financial security, she has no desire to grow her business beyond what she can comfortably manage alone.

Self-employment is empowering. A full one-quarter of the U.S. workforce—a segment comprised of more than 21.7 million individuals—is currently categorized as self-employed.[1] This group includes business owners in addition to consultants, contractors, and temporary workers. Many of these business owners run small home-based businesses, and hence employ no additional workers, but they nevertheless make plenty of significant contributions to our country's culture and economy. I also recognize that many great companies have sprung from the simple objective, or maybe out of the necessity, of being one's own boss. But this book is meant to speak primarily to those who share Lisa's vision. Whether or not you will seek venture capital or borrow from Mom and Dad; whether or not your new business will ever place you solidly among the ranks of the self-employed; whether you're starting in your garage with a laptop or in an expansive space at the top of a glittering urban high-rise—if you're dreaming big, I consider you an entrepreneur. If you have visions of changing the world and you see no limitations on the horizon of your venture, then you, by *my* definition, are an entrepreneur.

Back in 2003, I can distinctly remember reading the famous *Inc. 500* magazine issue that showcases the 500 fastest growing privately-held companies in the United States. Right then and there I made it a personal goal to have a company that ranked in the Inc. 500. Given the fact that at the time, my company was only about two years old and wasn't earning anywhere near the minimum requirement of $1M in revenue, it was a pretty audacious goal. Plenty of naysayers told me it couldn't be done. But the upstart in me refused to give up my dream. In 2007, when we reached number 247 on the Inc. 500 with a three-year growth rate of almost 1000%, I was ecstatic, but not surprised.

The same entrepreneurial spirit that motivates me, my friend Lisa, and my idols Michael Dell and Richard Branson is inextricably woven into our national fabric and has been part of the American dream from the beginning of our country's history. The rags-to-riches stories of icons like John D. Rockefeller and Andrew Carnegie and the creative legacies of innovators like Benjamin Franklin, Thomas Edison, and Henry Ford have inspired generations of would-be entrepreneurs. And there is no indication that the dream is dying. According to the U.S. Department of Commerce, over 600,000 new businesses start operations every year. Despite being a disastrous year for the economy, 2008 nevertheless saw the launch of more than 627,000 new startups.[2] And in 2009, in the midst of deep recession and record levels of unemployment, the incidence of newly launched businesses reached the highest level in 14 years, exceeding even the number of startups that took off during 1999-2000 (the peak years of the technology boom).[3] If you're considering the allure of entrepreneurship, you're certainly not alone.

If you're thinking that half of these annual startups fail in the first year, you're not alone there, either. This shockingly high failure rate for new businesses has long been a persistent misconception among the American business world. The facts are actually a lot more encouraging. The latest statistics from the Small Business Administration (SBA) show that two-thirds of new employer establishments survive at least two years, and 44% survive at least four years. Brian Head, economist with the SBA Office of Advocacy, noted that these latest statistics are a far more accurate assessment of new business success rates, and that, generally speaking, new employer businesses (those that employ other people) have about a 50/50 chance of surviving beyond their first five years.[4]

These fairly favorable success rates are a cause for optimism, of course, but the fact remains that a significant number of new businesses do indeed fail. Launching a new business is still risky and takes courage, as the risks can never be completely eliminated. In fact, as most any entrepreneur would tell you—certainly any serial entrepreneur—the risk is part of the fun. An entrepreneur relishes challenge. He or she will likely view problems and obstacles as invigorating and see that risky gray area of uncertainty as exactly the place where the success, and the wealth, potentially lies. For the classic entrepreneurial personality, that 50/50 survival rate I cited above illustrates a cup half full rather than one half empty. But a clear-eyed willingness to accept risk is not at all the same thing as reckless gambling. The reasons why businesses fail might seem unlimited, but there really is just a handful of forces at work, one of the most common of these being undercapitalization. But there are also plenty of redundancies on the lists of why businesses *succeed*, and that's where we should focus.

As I've said, for entrepreneurs, the risks can't be eliminated. But a little groundwork, a little homework, and a lot of soul-searching can reduce them considerably. Once you've identified your strengths and weaknesses, you can better assess your readiness for entrepreneurship. There are objective methods for analyzing a good business opportunity, and similarly, there are ways to avoid the most common pitfalls that crop up during the early decision stages. There is a nexus between the demands for financing and for growth that can be found and sustained as your business expands. Finally, you can tap a valuable store of information and advice for ongoing assistance. None of this knowledge or these resources will make a venture absolutely foolproof. But they can keep you from jumping blind when you take the leap, and they'll make you considerably more informed and prepared when starting your own business.

My hope is that my own experiences, as well as the stories that colleagues and peers have shared with me as a result of my work with entrepreneurial organizations, will be helpful to aspiring and existing entrepreneurs. If you're thinking about entrepreneurship, I want to encourage you. If you're already an entrepreneur, perhaps one who's hit some of that inevitable choppy sea in your voyage, I hope you will find something in these pages to support and sustain you. And if you're the spouse or significant other, family member, or friend of a budding business owner, perhaps this book will help you demystify that entrepreneurial personality so you can better understand how he or she ticks, and why he or she thinks that starting one's own business is the challenge—and the thrill—of a lifetime.

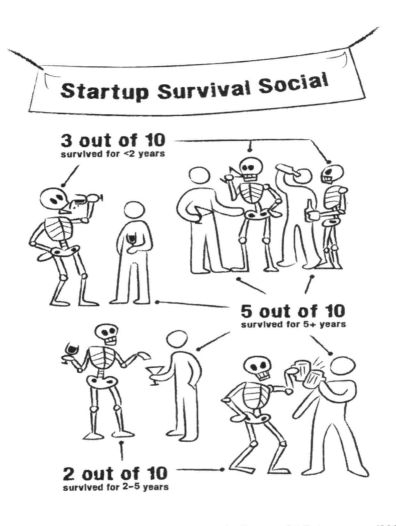

From Kauffman Foundation study, *Anatomy of a Successful Entrepreneur* (2009)

CHAPTER 1 ▪ DO YOU HAVE WHAT IT TAKES?

The reasons why would-be entrepreneurs take the plunge are probably as varied as the businesses they start. But how much do someone's inborn traits affect their success at starting a business? Countless popular books and volumes of academic research have been devoted to exploring the cluster of personal dispositions that make up the entrepreneurial mindset. While I agree that certain traits are helpful, I don't think that personality is the end-all-be-all determinant of success. I don't think there is a single ideal entrepreneurial "type" that excels to the exclusion of all others, nor is there any set of experiential or educational prerequisites that an entrepreneur must have. I don't think you need an MBA, tons of management experience, or serious capital. In fact, I'd wager that for most entrepreneurs, it's about a 30/70 split: 30% of their success comes from inborn personality traits that help them excel, and 70% comes from things that can be learned or acquired through experience. If you don't have all the ideal personality traits, you can still make up for it in other areas. For example, as countless startup entrepreneurs have demonstrated, an unusually strong drive may well compensate for a lack of experience.

But all that being said, I can affirm with equal conviction that owning a business isn't for everybody. As Bill Rancic, winner of the first season of Donald Trump's TV show *The Apprentice*, put it, "If it really was a no-brainer to make it on your own in business, there'd be millions of no-brained, harebrained, and otherwise dubiously brained individuals quitting their day jobs and hanging out their own shingles. Nobody would be left to round out the workforce and execute the business plan."[5] So while entrepreneurs aren't always born that way, it still takes a special sort of person to be a successful entrepreneur.

So what exactly does it take to be an entrepreneur? What qualities should a successful entrepreneur have? Here are some of the essential traits and characteristics I think are crucial.

➢ *Energy and Good Health*

Many business failures have come about because of the founder's poor health, and far too many new entrepreneurs simply underestimate the physical demands of starting and running a business. Breaking the mold of the 40-hour work week may not be one of your ultimate goals of starting a business. Actually, as I'll discuss later, working nontraditional hours can be an enjoyable byproduct of working for yourself, but you're probably not going to have much flexibility or time off—if any at all—in the beginning. I'm also not saying that you need to be a triathlon athlete, or even especially young. As a matter of fact, the second-largest growth jump in business creation rates last year was in the 55-64 year-old age group.[6] But most new ventures are extraordinarily work and time-intensive, particularly at the very beginning. The schedule can be pretty grueling, to say the least.

Being an entrepreneur means being your own boss, but it also means working harder than you ever have before, and for longer hours (at least at first). So if you're considering starting a company because you want to set your own schedule or have more free time, just be aware that it might be a while before you a reach that point.

➤ *Egotism and Confidence*

Entrepreneurs are a pretty egotistical bunch. It's not that they're megalomaniacs, although they often have some pretty grandiose ideas. Nor do I mean to suggest that they don't have fears or ever entertain doubts. It's just that their own self-confidence easily overrides fear and doubt. They know they can do it, and this frame of mind sets them up for achievement. As the title of this book reflects, they are what we frequently term "upstarts" in that they're a little presumptuous, or even audacious, in their self-confidence. That small voice inside them tends to speak more clearly than the voices of others, even those of "experts." While some might consider this a character flaw, it is actually an essential ingredient in any entrepreneurial success story.

People told Henry Ford he was crazy when he wanted to mass produce the automobile. Fred Smith's college paper, which outlined the plans for the shipping service that would later become FedEx, received a C from his professor on the grounds that it was not a viable business idea.[7] For many years, Clarence Birdseye failed to convince skeptical consumers that frozen food could be healthy and delicious, even going bankrupt several times in the process. Eventually, his quick-freeze technique caught on and became the benchmark for an entirely new industry. All of these guys were upstarts in their own right.

They ignored their detractors and stayed focused and driven. In fact, like most entrepreneurs, they were actually energized and spurred on by people telling them that they would fail. And now just look at how reliant we've become on cars, overnight shipping, and microwave meals!

Entrepreneurs simply *must* have a healthy confidence in their own judgment and abilities. If you find yourself demoralized by the blank look on your friends' faces when you try to explain your idea, or if you'll be completely deflated when countless potential investors or clients turn you down time and time again, you might want to reconsider.

➤ *Passion and Enthusiasm*

If there's one recurring theme in the biographies of great American entrepreneurs, it's passion. Your passion will be the propelling force that moves your business forward as the contagion of your enthusiasm quickly creates converts who share your excitement about your product or service. In the emotionally charged and physically challenging atmosphere of an embryonic business, it's passion that's going to get you over hurdles and through slowdowns, ultimately sustaining your business and protecting you from burnout.

If you find it difficult to get excited about your venture—or if you're generally the sort of person who just doesn't get too fired up about things—and if you're not comfortable with self-promotion, you may have a tough time infecting people with your enthusiasm and selling your vision to others.

➤ *Flexibility and Openness to Change*

Entrepreneurs are not merely agents of change in the marketplace and the world, but they themselves are exceptionally good at handling change. In the typical startup, you will have to be multitasking all the time, which will require you to wear many different hats in the space of a single day. When I started my first company, Hannon Hill, I was the software programmer, support team, salesman, and marketing department, all rolled into one. Successful entrepreneurs must be agile enough to jump back and forth between different roles and duties depending upon what the business needs most at any given moment. As the business grows, they must be flexible enough to realize when market or economic conditions have changed, and they should be able to determine when it's time to call in qualified reinforcements, to delegate responsibilities, or to hand the reins over to others. The best company founders will respond quickly to changing conditions, revising, shifting, tweaking, and adjusting their goals and strategies accordingly. Sometimes this might even involve completely reinventing their business and taking an entirely new path without losing their overarching vision. This takes a nimble personality—someone who is confident enough to act quickly on a hunch and change course completely if conditions necessitate it. This incremental shape-shifting process known as *iteration* is a healthy thing for every startup, and I'll refer to it throughout this book. While it happens far less often than iteration, *pivoting* involves making far more drastic or decisive changes, and you also have to be prepared for this possibility. As I see it, this willingness to change, and the good sense to recognize when it's time to do so, are fundamental to entrepreneurial success.

If you have a deeply ingrained aversion to risk or fear of change, or if you're easily derailed when pulled off task, you might want to reconsider the prospect of business ownership.

➢ *Persistence and Determination*

Hard-headed. Stubborn. Single-minded. Obsessed. Call it what you will, but as unflattering as these terms might sound, unfailing determination in some form definitely belongs on this list. Like the shark that must keep swimming or die, the classic entrepreneurial type knows that he or she must continually move forward in order to keep the business alive. Sometimes this may require moving in an entirely new direction, as I mentioned above. Occasionally, it may even mean slowing down for a little while. But you can never quit moving altogether, nor can you allow obstacles or uncertainty to stop your progress.

Ask any entrepreneur who has "made it" and you're bound to get a personal story about overcoming great obstacles through sheer determination. In fact, I've got one such story of my own. In the fall of 2003, the company I had founded was almost out of money. We had $50K in credit card debt, and we were just a couple of weeks away from being forced to lay off our employees, close our doors, and get "real" jobs. Any reasonable person might have thrown in the towel, cut their losses, and walked away. But it never once occurred to me to give up. I knew I had what it takes to succeed, and I knew that I had come too far just to give up and retreat. Failure was simply not an option.

If you have trouble with follow-through, are often told that you give up too easily, cannot make decisions without having 100% of the data, or frequently experience paralysis in the face of uncertainty, you may find that business ownership is best left to others.

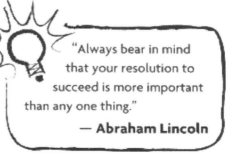

"Always bear in mind that your resolution to succeed is more important than any one thing."

— **Abraham Lincoln**

As promised, my list is a relatively abbreviated one. Some might argue that I've left out some of the key traits that people expect successful entrepreneurs to have. For instance, I didn't say anything about being good with numbers, possessing a sales-friendly personality, or having a technology background. All of these things are helpful, of course, but they are not make-or-break attributes that every successful entrepreneur must have, and in most cases, they can be learned. If you're lacking in any of these areas (finance, sales, technology, etc.), you'll find workarounds in the complementary attributes of carefully selected cofounders, partners, and team members. In listing the traits above, I wanted to focus on what I consider to be the basics of the entrepreneurial temperament.

In evaluating your own strengths and weaknesses, it helps to talk to other entrepreneurs and colleagues, as well as with the friends and family members who know you best. If getting career counseling or a life coach is an option for you, then by all means, go for it! There are also some good tools and questionnaires available that should help you assess your readiness to become an entrepreneur. A great place to start is with the assessment tool on the Small Business Association (SBA) site, although there are plenty of other resources out there that you might also find helpful. But my guess is that if you've truly been bitten by the entrepreneurial bug, you won't need a tool to tell you so.

In the final analysis, you probably already know whether or not you have what it takes to make it as an entrepreneur. If you're a healthy, energetic, self-confident person who manages change well, can get enthusiastically fired up in the right circumstances, and knows from experience that you can keep forging onward even in the face of obstacles and uncertainty, then entrepreneurship is for you.

CHAPTER 2 ▪ WHAT'S YOUR PROBLEM?

At the core of every great business idea is a problem. Perhaps it first surfaced as your own problem. *How can I do this? What will meet this need? What's a better way? How can I get from here to there?* People's problems, and the need for solutions to them, frequently provide the spark that ignites invention and innovation. To paraphrase countless business-driven motivational speakers: "Money is the reward you receive for solving a problem."

Fortunately, there are plenty of problems to go around. If you can identify a problem and solve it more efficiently, easily, cheaply, or quickly than your competition, then you already have one of the most fundamental components of a successful business in place. Sounds easy, right? Well, there's a bit more to it than that.

IDENTIFYING A PROBLEM TO SOLVE

There are countless stories of regular people becoming entrepreneurs simply because they had a problem that needed solving. Richard Drew of the 3M Company noticed some auto detailers complaining about messy two-tone painting and solved that problem by inventing masking tape. Kinko's copy shops came into being when a student at the University of Southern California, Paul Orfalea, learned the hard way that photocopying was expensive and inaccessible. VMWare founder Diane Greene wanted to solve the problem of having too many physical computers to manage, so she came up with a way that a single physical computer can contain many virtual ones, making it much easier to troubleshoot and move virtualized computers to another physical machine if there's a hardware issue.

The point is this: Good ideas don't usually just come to people in a vacuum. Solving problems inspires invention and drives innovation. Keep this in mind as you witness your own entrepreneurial impulses evolve into marketable ideas. As a software entrepreneur with my head in the Cloud, it's easy to forget that many business ideas come from tangible solutions to commonplace problems. I recently met two entrepreneurs who invented physical products—both sleep-related products, one geared towards adults and the other for kids. In both cases, they came up with their respective ideas solely because they wanted to solve their own unique problems. It just so happened that there were already markets for their products because plenty of other people were also looking to solve the same problems.

Aside from all of the problems that can be tackled offline with physical solutions, the rise of technology has created a wealth of new conundrums that must be addressed in the digital world. Ross Perot created Electronic Data Systems (EDS) because he saw that large companies needed computer data processing help if they were going to be able to take full advantage of emerging technology. Google and YouTube are two more contemporary—not to mention conspicuous—examples of technological answers to technological needs. Marketing automation, the technology behind one of my own companies, was developed to track and nurture sales leads. Skype has solved the pain point of having to pay astronomical rates for international telephone calls by enabling free calling via the web. PayPal, another free service, solved the high-risk problem of making online money transfers.

Solving a problem, whether online or offline, is a great starting place for entrepreneurs. That said, be sure you don't end up aiming to solve a problem that doesn't exist. You don't need to

"It's not that I'm so smart, it's just that I stay with problems longer."
— **Albert Einstein**

invent a problem by dreaming up unlikely scenarios and proposing the solution. Stick to solving real problems and you'll be on the right track.

DIFFERENTIATING YOURSELF

If your new business product or service will be what management guru Peter Drucker called *innovative*, it will solve a problem that no one else has successfully addressed. Most businesses, however, are to some degree *replicative*, in that they're in competition with other companies to solve the problems they're working on. Innovative companies simply have to create something new and exciting. Replicative businesses must work much harder to be different because they are in a sense reinventing the wheel. The world probably doesn't need yet another widget. But it might just need the best widget ever created, the cheapest widget, the widget that gets there fastest, or the widget that comes with a money-back guarantee and world-class customer service. I'm talking about old-fashioned competitive advantage here—the ability of your product or service, through some unique feature or specialization, to perform at a higher level than its competitors.

To differentiate yourself sufficiently, your product or service needs to excel in one or more of the following areas:

➤ *Quality*

The notion of quality is to a large extent a subjective attribute, perceived differently by different people. For some people, quality may be defined by the absence of defects or the extent to which a product outperforms or outlasts the competition. In engineering and manufacturing processes, it is the measure by which a product meets target specifications. But for most of us, quality strongly correlates with customer satisfaction and can be objectively measured through focus groups, surveys, and endorsements—but, most crucially, by sales.

A new business, even without having much of a track record, can begin building a unique selling position around quality in several different ways. One way might be by bragging about the experience or track record of principals (e.g., *one hundred years of combined experience in xyz*). Another approach is to use guarantees and warranties to corroborate the stated quality of your service or product. Craftsman Tools started as a store sub-brand of Sears in the 1920s, and it quickly made itself a household name by offering a lifetime warranty on all of its tools. Sony built an empire in the 1980s by touting the dependability and quality construction of its electronics. Briggs and Riley make quality luggage that carries a lifetime guarantee and hence has become the first choice of airline crews and frequent flyers. These brands remain relevant today, largely due to their reputation for quality.

Establishing quality as a selling strength can be difficult because it takes time for a business to prove that it can consistently meet the expectations of its customers. But making quality a priority and promoting it as a selling position remains one of the most powerful ways to enter (and eventually dominate) a market; once established, a reputation for quality is an enduring and self-perpetuating distinction. Honda has built its brand by promoting the quality and dependability of its cars, so it's not surprising that it has been the #1 choice of consumers for many years running, consistently ranking at the top of surveys on these same attributes. An established reputation for quality is a profoundly powerful thing.

➢ *Service*

The internet has so raised consumer expectations for good service that things that were once differentiators—fast and accurate order fulfillment, flexible shipping, and friendly follow-up—have become *de rigueur* for most companies' service departments. And because the web is open for business 24/7/365, it is harder than ever for companies, especially traditional brick-and-mortar businesses, to brush off or ignore customer complaints. The customer controls the message now with blogs and other social media serving as an instantaneous platform for customer dialogue to go public. Reviews (good and bad alike) can be posted and shared with potentially millions of other consumers, all with the click of a mouse. Needless to say, this shift to web commerce has set the customer service bar quite high.

An instructive example here is the viral video of an original song called "United Breaks Guitars." When United customer Dave Carroll's guitar was broken during a flight and United refused to do anything about it, Dave got mad. Then Dave wrote a song about his frustrating experience with the poor customer service he had received, filmed himself singing the song, and posted the video to YouTube. It was an overnight sensation and quickly became an iTunes hit as well. The video was a disaster for United, who moved quickly to address Dave's issue and ultimately ended up changing its policy to be more customer-friendly. The lesson here is to never underestimate the power of one dissatisfied customer with internet access.

Fortunately, though, while it has raised the standard for customer service considerably, the internet has also supplied the means to provide better service than ever before. Customer service websites, email autoresponders, comprehensive FAQs, live chat, aftermarket support, and similar tools, when executed well, enable a level of customer service that is not merely adequate, but exceptional. Amazon.com regularly tops the list for best customer service in the annual survey by The National Retail Federation and American Express.[8] While Amazon provides help desk telephone support, it's rarely needed because the site's comprehensive automated help tools are so effective. A titan of customer service, Zappos, has inspired consumer confidence and loyalty with their notoriously liberal "no questions asked" return policy. It's also worth mentioning here that both of these companies are online retailers as well as perennial growth stories.

It might sound a bit hackneyed, but it is definitely true that one of the simplest and best ways to differentiate your startup is through providing outstanding customer service. The benefits will come not only from customer retention, but also from employee satisfaction—and, subsequently, employee retention. People want to work for organizations that truly care about their customers; make this a cornerstone of your hiring process and corporate culture, and you're sure to foster a climate of excellent customer service. Zappos is probably the most conspicuous example of this, with excellent customer service and exuberantly evangelical employees to match. As a result of this winning combination, Zappos has managed to win over not just loyal customers but devoted, evangelical fans.

➢ *Pricing*

In the case of a highly innovative business or an emerging industry, it can be fairly easy, at least for a while, to make price your unique selling position. Becoming the low-cost leader in a replicative business is much harder because this positioning is dependent on low costs and high sales volume. Lose ground in either of those areas and you're no longer the low-cost leader. An alternative way to create a pricing advantage is to leverage a more efficient, economical production method or process, even with something as simple as strategic inventory strategies. If you have a revolutionary new, cost-effective, or low-waste way to manufacture widgets—through the use of robotics, for example—you've addressed the pricing paradigm. But there are even more creative ways to think about different pricing strategies, particularly for web startups and especially in relation to what is in the market already. Some common examples come to mind:

- Have monthly contracts instead of annual ones (unlike cable and cell phone companies).

- Provide an unconditional, money-back guarantee (like CarMax).

- Only charge if a transaction was successful (like Google Pay Per Action or eBay Motors).

- Offer free trials or "freemium" products (like MailChimp, Spotify, and Hulu). The freemium model provides the most basic version of a product or service for free to casual or new users, while generating revenue by charging advanced users for additional features or functionality.

- Offer discounting and promotion off a list price that's comparable to, or above, the competition's. Remember that it's always easy to lower your prices, but it's much harder to convince your customers or prospects why you must raise your product's price.

- Use the Gillette razor blade model. Sell cheaply, or give away, one product in order to ensure recurring sales of an essential related product at a much higher price. Manufacturers of inkjet printers and e-book readers have found great success generating revenue this way.

- Simply offer your customers better terms than your competitors do.

The point here is that there is more than one way to think about pricing, and there are multiple approaches to making price your unique strength position. By building these pricing strategies into the business model from day one, the company adapts and grows around them such that the company's long-term interests stay closely aligned with those of its customers.

➢ *Delivery*

Some companies have placed emphasis on reliability and quick delivery of a product or service, while others pride themselves on providing an excellent customer experience for each and every transaction. One great example of stellar delivery is Uber.com, a taxi service for smartphone users. Summon a cab using this entirely electronic service and you'll immediately see the emphasis on delivery. The app counts down to when your taxi will arrive, and it also shows the car overlaid on a map so that you can see where it is relative to your current location. This is delivery at its finest.

The Zappos creed of "wowing" customers also fits into this theme of spectacular delivery. Want a pair of shoes right away? Place an order on Zappos and you'll be wearing them in a matter of days. Don't like the shoes? Use their free returns service for an exchange or refund. It's hard to beat delivery terms like these, and they make the overall customer experience that much better.

FINDING YOUR NICHE

To the extent that you can distinguish or differentiate your

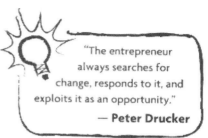

"The entrepreneur always searches for change, responds to it, and exploits it as an opportunity."
— **Peter Drucker**

company on the basis of one or more of the paradigms discussed above—quality, service, pricing, or delivery—your likelihood of success will increase drastically. To cite one ubiquitous example, McDonald's single-handedly invented the fast food industry when founder Ray Kroc combined the consumer virtues of speedy delivery and friendly service with low prices. One of my own companies, Pardot, has become successful by focusing on ease of delivery and outstanding customer service. Our product, a robust marketing automation tool, is classified as software as a service, or *SaaS*. By using the subscription-based SaaS delivery model, we offer a product that brings affordable lead management and marketing automation capabilities to an underserved market: small and medium-sized businesses. From the beginning, we have sought to differentiate ourselves by providing our clients with unsurpassed customer service and support. We also promote transparency by making publicly available resources like our pricing structure, knowledge base, white papers, and helpful tips and links. Our services team responds via phone or email to each and every customer question or request in less than fifteen minutes on average. Standards like these are important to uphold, of course, but the real secret of our success is the human element—all of the great folks we hire and train to go above and beyond. We provide our customers with awesome support from friendly, knowledgeable people, and in return, our customers love us and stay loyal.

The takeaway here is that finding your competitive advantage is a balancing act. You should never focus on only one of these elemental components to the exclusion of all others, particularly if the customer suffers as a result. As marketing strategist Tara Hunt has quipped, "designing your product for monetization first and people second will probably leave you with neither."[9] At the same time, it is unrealistic to think you can be all things to all people all of the time. Tim Berry, president and founder of Palo Alto Software, puts it this way:

> You can't do everything. In restaurants, you can't credibly offer great food at bargain prices with great atmosphere. If you say you do, nobody believes you anyhow. So you have to focus. Make this focus intertwined and enmeshed with your choice of key target customer and your own business identity.[10]

I'm by no means suggesting that in the early stages of a startup, you should already have a perfectly clear focus or a developed business identity. I do believe, however, that your chances for success will improve significantly as you become clearer on who you are (identity) and what you do (focus). Taken together, these things help you find where you belong (niche).

Apple offers an instructive example here. Apple has carefully cultivated one of the strongest and most enduring brand identities out there: hip, young, fresh, progressive, forward-thinking. Combine this unambiguous identity with Apple's product focus—high-quality computers and consumer electronics with dazzling user interfaces—and you have a winning combination. Apple's ongoing popularity and die-hard fan base are testament to just how successful this company has been in leveraging this equation to its great benefit.

In order for your dream to be different—in order to achieve that competitive advantage you need to succeed—your entry strategy will necessarily need to prioritize your strengths and focal points. Be thinking about how you will highlight these strengths in your business model, how you will communicate them to potential customers or investors, and how your marketing strategy will support and exploit them. Make sure you can define and articulate how your focus is sharpened by your own experience (and that of other cofounders, if applicable). Entrepreneur-turned-venture capitalist Mark Suster calls this the "unfair advantage" and says it is exactly what he wants to hear about from the startup applicants he interviews and is the reason he likes for people who present to him to start with their personal bios. Advises Suster: "I want to know what unique experiences you bring to the table that are going to give your business a faster time to market, a better designed product, more knowledge of your customers' problems—a higher likelihood of success."[11] Look within yourself and you will likely get a head start on identifying the strengths that will determine your company's competitive advantage and its future success.

PUTTING YOURSELF OUT THERE

The Internet Age has so altered the concept of delivery that we almost need a new word for what has transpired. It has revolutionized news delivery in an overwhelmingly positive sense, yet at the same time, it has created an identity crisis for print journalism and will no doubt get the blame (or the credit, if you like) when the last print newspaper rolls off the presses. Similarly, the internet has radically and permanently altered the way we communicate with each other and has revolutionized the way we shop for almost everything. Music, books, clothing, groceries, vacations, financial products, engagement rings, and even college courses are routinely delivered via the web at the conclusion of a commercial transaction that took place entirely online. Even the public sphere has transformed into a virtual village green of sorts. Most of us can recall a time when chores like renewing your driver's license or taking care of a tax bill could only be accomplished by physically standing in line and paying with cash or check.

Despite its relatively young age, the internet has already become a global economic and cultural phenomenon. Over a decade ago, Bill Gates astutely foresaw the magnitude of the effects the World Wide Web would have on our way of life, saying, "Despite its impact, today's Internet is still roughly where the automobile was during the era of Henry Ford's Model T. We've seen a lot of amazing things so far, but there is much more to come. We are only at the dawn of the Internet Age."[12] Folks who study this stuff for a living are generally in agreement that similar innovations will continue to surprise and delight us. As a recent Pew Research Center poll on the future of the internet reveals, fully 80% of the experts polled thought that the devices and applications that emerge as game-changers in the next decade will more often than not come entirely, to use the survey's terminology, "out of the blue."[13]

Think for a moment about cloud computing. A few years ago, most people had never even heard of it, but pretty soon it will form the foundation of almost everything we do. Cloud computing represents a paradigm shift in the way we live our lives. It has gained popularity fast enough to have significantly affected modern life as we know it. Because cloud computing uses remote servers operating in a virtualized manner, its capacity for storing and processing data is essentially limitless. This has revolutionized what we can do online, as evidenced by everything from Wikipedia to iTunes. Browser-based applications are rapidly outstripping installed software in popularity and efficiency. Even the associated costs of doing things online have declined to the point of being inconsequential. Cloud computing, at least for now, is the wave of the future.

When it comes to thinking about the internet and its related innovations, and how all of this affects the way in which you put yourself and your business out there, here are a few things to ponder:

- Will the certainty of cheaper and more powerful computers and the proliferation of high-speed internet access and cloud computing have a positive or adverse effect on my business?

- Is there any likelihood that my physically delivered product or service will be eclipsed by virtual delivery?

- Will my business be oriented toward (and deliver consumables to) the customer who is not web-savvy?

- Am I committed to keeping current on and utilizing new technologies that make for the fastest and most efficient delivery of goods, services, or information to my customers?

- Can I gather the knowledge necessary to exploit the internet marketing tools available for growing my business?

- Will I take full advantage of the social media channels through which my customers may be talking to each other and to my competitors, possibly about my company?

- Am I willing to open my business up to the crowd, soliciting feedback and ideas on how to improve my product, its delivery, and my company's customer service, or do I prefer to follow the prescribed orthodoxy?

What this means for entrepreneurship more generally, even if you're not a web entrepreneur, is that the internet is truly a force to be reckoned with. It's not going to go away, and you can't simply bypass it; it is forever changing the way we live and do business. Entrepreneurs can either learn to harness it to our advantage or be blindsided by what we're not paying attention to, risking our own obsolescence. As you'll hear me argue again and again, every business today is in some way an e-business. If it's not, it had better become one fast. Adapt or die!

CHAPTER 3 ▪
SHOW ME THE MONEY

The typical entrepreneur starts worrying about money long before there's a solid idea, a management team, or even any operating history. But if you haven't given much thought to the details of how you'll go about funding your company, there are essentially three paths you can take:

1. Give up some of your company in return for the cash you need (equity financing),

2. Go into debt to get your start-up capital (debt financing), or

3. Bootstrap your way to success.

A fourth way that's far less common than the ones above is to find a strategic partner who is willing to pay you to build a product they need. While I already have a strong preference that I'll defend and advocate for later on, we should give fair treatment to each of the three options. In the following sections, we will cover the types and sources of investment capital and other financing options available to new businesses.

Equity Financing

Equity financing is built on the simple premise that you must give up something to get something. Typically, these arrangements require you to give up some of your company in return for the cash you need to grow your business. Equity financing often presents the most straightforward and direct path to the money, but there are certain caveats you should keep in mind. Whether you decide to deal with venture capitalists or angel investors, this is one common way to fund a startup.

Venture Capitalists

Venture capital (VC) and venture capitalists (VCs) have technically been around since 1958, when the U.S. Small Business Administration (SBA) began licensing small business investment companies (SBICs) to finance small entrepreneurial ventures.

However, the term and the practice didn't achieve popular understanding until the dot-com explosion in the late 1990s, when what seemed like an endless parade of Silicon Valley startups scored funding, grew like crazy, and finally went public—without profitability—making the major players temporarily wealthy beyond their wildest dreams.[*] Not every company followed this trajectory, but nevertheless it happened frequently enough that venture capital soon became part of the business financing mainstream.

While VCs may invest in a company at any stage of its growth, venture capital is best suited for companies with a breakthrough (or otherwise unique) product or service that has considerable national or international market potential. It's true that there's an exception to every rule, but here are the basics of what you need to know about venture capitalists:

- Venture capitalists are usually looking to invest in companies with extremely high growth potential; they typically invest amounts within the $1M-$15M range.

- In most cases, venture capital funding has a fixed lifespan of 7-10 years; occasionally there are funding extensions or funds that overlap.

- In return for their investments, VCs can generally expect to receive anywhere between 10-50% of the recipient company, with 25-35% being the most common

---

[*] For a good background on venture capital during the frenetic days of the internet boom in the late 1990s, check out the book *eBoys: The First Inside Account of Venture Capitalists at Work* by Randall Stross (Crown: 2000).

percentage.

- Short-term focus is key. VCs are not in it for the long haul and usually expect to harvest their returns within a timeframe of 3-7 years, with the expectation that the recipient company will either go public or be acquired by another company.

- VC firms tend to specialize by industry or market vertical. A software startup would likely hold little appeal to a firm that focuses on medical devices, for example.

- More often than not, VCs take a hands-on approach, actively monitoring and managing their business portfolios and exerting moderate to significant control over the company's management decisions. They usually get a seat on the board of directors, the right to approve significant investments, and so on.

One of the big advantages for traditional VCs is the opaque nature of information and the resulting frequency of negotiating deals. Think about it: a VC might negotiate a couple deals per year, while a successful entrepreneur might negotiate a few deals in a lifetime. Traditionally, limited access to information has given VCs the upper hand in these sorts of negotiations, but the more information that becomes available, the more efficient the market for VCs and entrepreneurs will be. While VCs will always have an advantage, the trend towards transparency and free access to information means that the dynamic is changing to be more equitable and far less heavily in favor of VCs than it used to be. So if VC funding seems like the right path for your company to pursue, don't be afraid to go that route.

Talking to VCs

If you decide to go the VC route, knowing where to start can be a daunting prospect, but there are some great resources to help you get started. The Center for Venture Research at the University of New Hampshire annually updates a comprehensive list of nationwide venture capital resources to help entrepreneurs in their networking process of finding early-stage capital. The list includes venture capital groups, venture forums, matching networks, and educational forums for entrepreneurs. Jens Lapinski also maintains an editable list of VC funds,[14] and there are plenty of other good databases out there.

Even if you aren't planning on raising money in the near term (or possibly ever), most entrepreneurs, particularly tech entrepreneurs, should still talk to VCs at some point. Why? Well, there are lots of reasons. Here are a few:

- Developing rapport with VCs early on in the game can prove to be very helpful in the event that you do decide to raise money in the future. The fundraising process can't be rushed; it typically takes twice as long as expected, so it helps to already have some introductions and discussions under your belt.

- VCs regularly encounter hundreds of businesses, thereby offering a sounding board, insight into trends, and advice on what works and what doesn't. If nothing else, think of your talks with VCs as information-gathering sessions that give you a chance to pick the brains of experienced individuals for valuable advice.

- VCs are generally very well-connected people. They can offer introductions to prospects, not to mention potential partners who could end up being invaluable to you down the road.

- VCs ask the tough questions, forcing you to make sure you understand the key performance indicators and metrics so that you can analyze your business more critically and objectively.

My recommendation is that you reach out to VCs and start developing relationships, even if you don't have current fundraising plans.

Angel Investors

Because of the tough requirements and high return expectations that venture capitalists have for potential investments, many entrepreneurs seek early funding from angel investors, who may be more willing to invest in highly speculative opportunities or may even have a prior relationship with the entrepreneur. The term "angel" was borrowed by the business community from Broadway, where it originally described those individuals who put up the money to back stage plays and other theatrical productions. Typically, angels are wealthy individuals and are often experienced entrepreneurs or business executives themselves. In recent years, angel investors have started banding together in networks or groups in order to share information and to pool resources such that they might extend their investment reach.

Just like with any investor, the profit motive certainly drives angels—in fact, angels are usually looking for higher returns than one might expect from a traditional investment. But that's not to say that idealistic or philanthropic impulses don't ever motivate angels and angel organizations. My own passion for startups and vision for helping make Atlanta a good place to start a company was my fundamental motivation in founding Shotput Ventures (now part of Georgia Tech-based Flashpoint), a technology startup accelerator fund that focuses on capital-light web services companies. We assist in the conception phase, provide significant mentoring and teaching, and often facilitate introductions to venture capitalists and other angel investors. The interest most angels have in startups usually goes beyond that of a traditional investor and includes some sort of passion or altruistic vision that entails helping like-minded entrepreneurs succeed. Shotput was born out of that vision.

Shotput Ventures/Flashpoint invests in early-stage companies that are located close to home (the Southeast U.S.), giving priority to startups who plan to headquarter permanently in the Atlanta area. A company with cofounders who are unwilling or unable to base themselves in or near Atlanta isn't automatically disqualified, but because one of our primary goals is to foster the growth of tech startups in the Atlanta area, location carries a lot of weight in our selection process. Aside from this crucial locational criterion, we also require participating companies to have two or more cofounders, one of whom must be a technical person.

We've gotten plenty of great applications at Shotput Ventures, but unfortunately we've had to pass on a number of promising companies because the applicants did not meet our stated requirements. Here are a few situations in which we learned lessons that helped us shape our entrance criteria:

- **The company only has one cofounder (or has too many).** It's next to impossible for one person to do everything well without having help. The opposite is also true: A team with too many cofounders is akin to having too many cooks in the kitchen. One of the teams we accepted in our inaugural class had five cofounders, and while they did gain some momentum, getting all of the cofounders on the same page was like herding cats. Our experience has shown us that teams of two or three people tend to be the most successful.

- **The company doesn't have a technical cofounder who is an experienced programmer.** Obviously this is crucial, given our stated preference for web-based businesses. One applicant we encountered had a really innovative idea and the business chops to make it happen, but he didn't have anyone to build his product. He actually asked us if we could help him find a technical cofounder, which suggested to us that as promising as his idea was, his company wasn't yet at the stage to be admitted to our program. For this reason, we require teams to have at least one technical cofounder.

- **Not all of the company's cofounders are willing or able to devote 100% of their time and effort to work on the new venture.** One of the first teams to graduate from the program had a cofounder living full-time in another state. This definitely complicated things for the team, which in turn created issues down the road. Far more often than not, day jobs and other obligations end up being detrimental to a startup's success, so this is why we want to ensure that participants are completely dedicated to working on the company and nothing else.

The bottom line is that a successful startup has to have more going for it than just a great idea. The team must be composed of bright and talented cofounders, who together will be completely consumed with making that idea happen. You're either dedicated and committed, or you're not.

Send Me an Angel

Even if you decide that your company is better suited to pursue the angel investor route, remember that it's never too early to begin building relationships. If you don't know anyone, you can start by checking out two especially good online listings of active angel individuals and networks in the U.S. and Canada. The Angel Capital Association is a professional alliance of 330 angel groups, and the Angel Capital Education Foundation, a nonprofit supported by the Ewing Marion Kauffman Foundation, lists about 200 angel networks. The Center for Venture Research website provides background data, average deal sizes, and profiles of angel characteristics and demographics.

But for reasons I've already mentioned, it might be easiest (and wisest) to just do your networking the old-fashioned way: Look for angels close to home. There are plenty of ways to do that, even if you're not sure where to start. Here are some suggestions for finding angels near you:

- **Leverage your resources.** Contact your local chamber of commerce to see if anyone knows of such a group. You can also talk to nearby business organizations and economic development agencies.

- **Ask around.** Inquire with financial and legal professionals (e.g., bankers, lawyers, accountants, et. al.) with whom you are already acquainted. They'll often have ties to the local angel investment community.

- **Go out and network.** Become a part of local networks with an industry-specific focus by attending events, meetings, and lectures where you'll find like-minded individuals. Getting involved is one of the best ways to meet angels, and you'll also benefit from interaction with your business peers.

- **Join the club.** Participate in groups with other entrepreneurs. I have gotten a great deal out of the ones I belong to, and you'll likely get similar benefits by joining your own group.

- **Get involved.** Startup catalysts and incubators are a great place to get involved in your local startup scene, and through your own involvement you'll likely have access to folks in the angel community. The Advanced Technology Development Center (ATDC) at the Georgia Institute of Technology is unquestionably the heart of Atlanta's tech startup scene; other cities likely have something similar.

These are all great ways to get out there and meet people. It's all about networking, and it can take longer than you think to develop relationships with angels and other influential people, so get started as early as you can.

VCs vs. Angels: What's the Difference?

Recently I was talking with an entrepreneur who was thinking about raising money. His technology startup is approaching the break-even point, and he sees a market opportunity to accelerate growth. We talked for a bit about his sales and marketing progress before delving into fundraising. After I asked about pre-money valuation, current revenue run rate, and the amount he wanted to raise, it became clear that he hadn't fully grasped the differences between raising money from angel investors vs. going to venture capitalists. I briefly summarized some of the key differences between the two as follows:

- Angels are typically more hands-off in their approach, while VCs usually take a seat on the board and are more hands-on.

- Angels are typically happy with a 3-5x return, while VCs

focus on opportunities that will yield 8-10x returns.

- Angels are typically satisfied with dividends providing some liquidity, while VCs want profits reinvested to maximize growth.

- Angels typically don't make huge investments, while VCs can provide significantly more equity.

- Angels typically don't make investments with as many strings attached (e.g., anti-dilution, liquidity preferences, etc.), compared to the conditional investments that are standard for VCs.

- Angels typically want to invest an amount they're comfortable with (say $50K) without budgeting for follow-on investment. VCs however, start with an amount (say $1M) and want to put more money to work in the same company in later rounds. Thus, taking the VC route means you must plan for several rounds of financing.

- Angels typically have more emotional motivations for investing, ones that go beyond the VC gold standard of investing based on the best management team. Business models and strategies can always be changed, but passionate and talented cofounders are hard to come by. Many angels like the mentoring aspect because it lets them "stay in the game" (from which they might have formally retired or exited).

My main point in discussing these differences is that it's important to be able to distinguish between VCs and angels before making any decisions about raising funds.

DEBT FINANCING

While nobody ever really enjoys the idea of creating more debt, most of us recognize that there are some things—an education, a home, unexpected medical expenses—for which incurring debt may be a necessary evil. Funding your startup may be one of these things. If this is the case, then debt financing might be an option for you. The advantage to debt financing is that it can let you keep your ownership interest intact while allowing for greater flexibility when combined with other types of financing. There are several different ways you can pursue debt financing.

Borrowing Against Assets

The federal law codified in the Employee Retirement Income Security Act (ERISA) of 1974 is structured so that you can invest your existing IRA or 401(k) funds in a business without suffering any penalties for early distribution. In today's economy, many entrepreneurs have greater faith in the growth opportunities of their own fledgling enterprise than in Wall Street, or at the very least, they see their own self-investment as a way to diversify some of their retirement holdings. Mortgaging property you own and borrowing against life insurance policies are other options for making a loan to yourself.

Credit Cards

I initially used credit cards to pay the bills when I started my first business over a decade ago. I even played the precarious game of applying for new cards that had no interest for the first X months and then transferring the balances from my previous high-interest cards in an effort to minimize the interest rate on the outstanding balance. Racking up fifty thousand dollars of credit card debt, as I ended up doing in the end, is definitely not for the faint of heart, and I wouldn't suggest it for most people, but it is often the only way to get access to money in the crucial early stages of your company. I'd recommend getting the startup going by doing whatever it takes—including using your credit cards, if you must. Don't feel bad about it, because you're not alone: Credit cards remain the most popular form of funding for new startups. In fact, I like to refer to Capital One as the nation's #1 small business investor.

SBA Loans

I'm astonished at how many would-be entrepreneurs, armed only with a great idea and a lot of enthusiasm, think that a friendly call on Uncle Sam's "business bank"—the Small Business Administration (SBA)—will secure their startup funding. Well, here's the bad news (and there's really no fancy way to package it):

1. The SBA does *not* lend money.

2. There are *no* government grants to help you start a for-profit business.

The SBA does sponsor and encourage several types of business loan programs, but they don't actually make the loans; they are merely the guarantor of those loans, and not the full guarantor at that. You'll actually have to pay a visit to your local commercial bank, armed with the same "3 Cs"—credit, character, and collateral—that you'd need if you were applying for any other loan.

I don't mean to be discouraging, but this is just the reality. If you're considering conventional bank financing and have the collateral to back it up, it's definitely worth your time to explore the SBA's options.

In addition to the SBA's basic 7(a) loan program, there are various specialty programs which include the following:

- The Community Express program is geared toward small businesses that plan to operate in underserved or distressed communities.

- The Patriot Express program is intended for companies in which veterans or active military control 51% or more of the company.

- A micro-loan program (for loans under $35K) is funded through non-profit based intermediaries.

- The CDC 504 program is available for companies that can qualify as Certified Development Companies.

To learn more about the Small Business Administration and its various programs, visit a SBA district office or take advantage of the wealth of resources provided at the SBA website.

Conventional Capital

Unfortunately, the primary source of low-interest loans for new small businesses—commercial and bank loans backed by the SBA's 7(a) program—has dried up significantly as of late as one of the many repercussions of the recent economic downturn. According to numbers released for the SBA's 2009 fiscal year, the 7(a) program made 36% fewer loans than it did in 2008, backing only 44,221 loans from banks for starting, purchasing, or expanding a small business.[15] According to data supplied by PricewaterhouseCoopers and the National Venture Capital Association, total VC dollars invested fell 39% between the first quarter of 2008 (before the recession began) and the first three months of 2010. Indeed, the entire conversation surrounding the scramble for private investment capital is an exercise in futility for most founders. Seeking out conventional capital to fund your startup has grown less and less attractive in the past few years. To put it bluntly: It's not impossible, but it sure isn't easy.

Friends and Family Funding

The dangers inherent in begging for money from your loved ones should be obvious, but the tremendously challenging task of securing institutional funding for the first-time entrepreneur may well tempt you to turn to family and friends for funds, just as one in ten novices do. Here's my best advice if you choose to go this route:

- **Be brutally honest.** And I do mean brutally. Be completely forthcoming with your friends or relatives about the nature of the business, the risks involved, and the timeline for payoff. Full disclosure is important in any financing agreement, but it's paramount when you're risking irreplaceable personal relationships.

- **Loans are preferable to equity arrangements.** If at all possible, structure your funding as a loan rather than as an equity arrangement. There are many advantages to this structure, but the most important one is that it won't entitle Uncle Harry to give you business advice on "his" startup.

- **Consider the worst-case scenario.** Don't take money from those who simply can't afford to lose it. Of course you're going to be successful. Of course you're going to repay the loan. But the worst-case scenario for any investor is that they will lose the whole enchilada. If you allow Mom and Dad to mortgage their home, do it with your eyes wide open, and be prepared for them to move in with you.

- **Don't forget that this is still a business arrangement.** Execute the same documents with friends and family that you would with a stranger. Make sure that all the legal *t's* have been crossed and the *i's* dotted. Handshakes, informal IOUs, or verbal assurances at a family reunion are great, but they're no substitute for crucial legal documents, which may also be important someday for tax or inheritance purposes. I recommend that every entrepreneur have a go-to lawyer; if you do not, consult an authoritative resource, such as the VirginMoney.com website, to read up on information about structuring social loans.

- **Keep them posted.** Once the agreement is in place, keep your friends or relatives informed of your business progress just as you would your board of directors. There's nothing wrong with informal updates given in person or over the phone, but maintain your professionalism by putting together a simple quarterly report assessing where you are with your startup business, what goals or milestones have been met, and so on. It's good practice for you, and your funders will appreciate the regular briefings.

While borrowing cash from the "Three Fs"—friends, family, and fools—certainly carries risks, plenty of businesses that were initially funded this way have ended up yielding positive (and often quite profitable) results. I tend to agree with Greg Boesel, CEO of Swaptree, Inc., who with cofounder Mark Hexamer has funded two companies by taking the Three Fs route. Boesel makes a compelling argument in favor of this funding model:

> If you are starting a company and you can't convince any of your friends and family that it is a business that has a chance of succeeding and that you are capable of doing everything necessary to make it a success, then you really shouldn't pursue it. If you can't convince your friends and family that your business is a good idea, you will never be able to convince an outside investor.[16]

BOOTSTRAPPING

If you decide to begin a business without external capital by funding your company's growth through internal cash flow, you'll be *bootstrapping.* Those who know me have heard me sing the praises of bootstrapping. I make no secret of the fact that this is my preferred method for getting a new company off the ground. I've done it, and it's worked well for me.

In my opinion, the majority of entrepreneurs shouldn't raise money, and 99% of entrepreneurs shouldn't raise money from institutional investors. But here are a few instances where raising money *does* make sense:

- There are some key mentors you would really like to be involved with the company, and they've offered to invest in exchange for a small stake in the company.

- The business is in a winner-take-all market, and if you aren't the leader, you'll likely be worthless (e.g., eBay for online auctions).

- The type of business you're beginning is incredibly capital-intensive or has high start-up costs and as such requires considerable early-stage investment in order to be successful (e.g., a medical device that requires special equipment to produce).

- From a lifestyle perspective (e.g., to support a growing family), you need to be able to pay yourself more than that below-market salary that typically sustains the new entrepreneur. It's a tough call, but a situation like this could require outside capital.

As you can see, there aren't too many compelling reasons to raise money, and it follows that most entrepreneurs probably shouldn't go this route. The fact is, the web has made it significantly cheaper to start and operate a company today than it was twenty—or even ten—years ago, before the internet revolution. Here are a few of the forces that have converged to make this possible:

- The falling costs of hardware and bandwidth
- The wider availability of open-source software
- The increasing ease and cost savings of working virtually
- Internet-based sales and marketing programs and other new technologies that enable more efficient and economical customer targeting
- Internet-based payment programs (and the decline in consumer concerns about the security of them)
- The rise of social media tools that enable wider and less expensive marketing reach

These developments have created entirely new economies of scale for startups, enabling even very small companies not only to operate, but to actually compete, worldwide. For that special class of entrepreneurs who can afford to live on next to nothing, who can budget carefully and watch the cash flows, and who are willing to do whatever it takes to succeed, there has never been a better time to give bootstrapping a go.

Bootstrapping buys you time to develop and mature your product or service at your own pace, free of the pressures from angels or VCs who want results in their time frame. It affords you complete creative control over your own brainchild and lets you develop your own business model, ensuring that any alterations and iterations are made for the right reasons: long-term growth and permanence, not short-term goals. Obviously, of all the ways you can fund your new venture, bootstrapping offers the most control over your destiny, as well as your profits—because even those first trickles of profit are yours alone, and you alone decide how much of them to reinvest. Finally, bootstrapping enhances your ability to get investor attention down the road, when your bootstrapped startup has a track record and you're ready to take it to the next level. For VCs and angels, nothing gets the funding green light like a proven track record of success.

Going forward, you'll find that that this book was written with a bootstrapper's mentality. The assumption is that you want to make money, not burn it. Even if you get VC capital or angel funding immediately, I hope that my suggestions and the shared experiences of others will still be useful as you progress through the stages of your startup.

CHAPTER 4 ▪ DRAFTING A DREAM TEAM

That old saying about two heads being better than one seems like a given when it comes to startups. Besides the fact that there's almost too much work for just one person to do alone, the startup process can often be lonely and isolating. I've been a solo founder as well as a cofounder, and I can honestly say that I prefer the cofounder route. I've found that I want the companionship and moral support, the sounding board, and certain core competencies that only other cofounders can provide.

But another old adage, the one that says "too many cooks spoil the stew," holds a good bit of wisdom for me also. Technology companies need to be fast and nimble, and having more people involved doesn't always make you faster. In fact, more often than not, having too many cofounders in the kitchen early on actually slows things down more. I have always found it crucial to be able to iterate on a product quickly, without changes or innovations having to go through the red tape and politics of consensus decision-making. There's a lot of debate out there about the ideal number of founders, but I have found that the ideal startup "stew" requires no more than two or three cofounder "cooks." And while all of you will be able to pick up skills on the job, at least one of you had better know how to cook or you risk getting burned in the kitchen.

THE COFOUNDER COMPLEMENT

When seeking out cofounders for a new business, the immediate temptation is to begin looking for someone very much like yourself—someone who shares the same interests, views the world much as you do, and is fun to be around. I think this can be a serious mistake, because it frequently results in the duplication of resources, recurring tasks and responsibilities that neither of you want to take on, and paralysis when it's time to make tough decisions.

Obviously, your cofounders should be people you genuinely like and whose company you enjoy. Especially in the early days of your startup, you'll likely spend more time with each other than with friends, family, or even spouses. Clearly your personalities should be compatible if you're going to be spending so much time together, often under challenging circumstances. But when it comes to founding and growing a business, your differences will probably end up being more important than your similarities. Google cofounders Larry Page and Sergey Brin reportedly disagreed about almost everything from the moment they met, yet they still managed to build a dynamic and extremely successful company.[17]

Before you build out your senior team, you need to inventory your own strengths and weaknesses. Be honest with yourself and acknowledge the weaknesses you'll need help overcoming. Ideally, you and your cofounder should bring complementary attributes to the table—personal qualities and acquired skills that are cooperative but not overlapping, and strengths that make up for each other's deficiencies. I like to call these attributes *cofounder complements*. Here are some examples (note that these aren't necessarily opposites):

- Her experience is technical; yours is in sales and marketing.

- His background is in finance; yours is in programming.

- She provides the vision; your strength lies in details and execution.

- His approach is assertive and bold; you're more relaxed and collaborative.

- She's fearless about success; you view the future with a measure of concern. (One cofounder is often an inveterate optimist, so a dose of reality doesn't hurt.)

- He's a natural salesperson; you're technology-focused. (This may be the golden complement.)

- She's passionate about your idea; you can't stop talking about your idea. (Everyone needs this shared enthusiasm!)

It's worth completing an honest self-analysis and spending sufficient time getting to know your potential collaborators so that you end up working with a motivated cofounder who brings complementary skills and attributes to your startup.

Technically Speaking

I was recently talking with a "napkin stage" (idea only) entrepreneur about his business when we got to the product portion of the conversation. Interestingly, he told me he didn't have a technical person yet on his two-person team, but that they had talked to some programmers who would build the web application he and his cofounder had designed. This revelation immediately sent up a red flag in my mind because I've always argued that it's imperative to have at least one technical cofounder on the team from the get-go. There are plenty of reasons why this is the case, but I'll highlight the most crucial ones below.

Bringing a technical founder on to join your team, as opposed to outsourcing your programming and technical needs, will give your startup the ability to iterate faster on the product. An in-house technical person provides valuable insight as far as product direction is concerned. In addition, having a technical cofounder means that time zone differentials and formal project protocols won't stand in the way of getting your problem solved or your glitch fixed—right here and right now, when your customer needs it. The company that is most responsive to the customer usually wins in the end. You can't be as responsive as you'd like when you're outsourcing the fundamentals of your product.

The onsite presence of your technical person can also add value when it comes to customer communication. We all remember playing the childhood game of "telephone" and seeing how easy it is for a bit of information or simple instructions to get garbled beyond recognition after being passed through just a few intermediaries. Well, a technical cofounder can keep you from playing that game. The fact that you can have a knowledgeable technical person on hand to talk *directly* to potential customers or actual users, bypassing the sales rep or the sales engineer entirely, will eliminate misunderstandings, wasted time, and frustration on both ends.

By the same token, having a technical person with a vested interest in seeing the company succeed effectively acts as a watchdog over your long-term goals and the alignment of your incentives. No consultant is going to be obsessing about your company's future; they are paid to complete a project, and nothing more. No consultant will know how to delicately weigh the customer's need for feature requests (and instant gratification) against the long view and vision of product functionality that fits your business model. A technical cofounder can help avoid these unfortunate pitfalls by keeping your product focused—or as I like to think of it, "opinionated."

The *absence* of a technical founder, on the other hand, can have negative connotations for potential investors, who may worry about the entrepreneur who wasn't able to sell the vision to a technical person and entice her to join the team, not to mention disastrous repercussions for future technical hires, who will join the company having no predecessor to turn to for necessary cues and clarifications. Personally, I'd be very reluctant to invest in a software company without a technical cofounder, and I'd worry about the outcome when such a company attempts to build out a headless engineering team.

The absence of a technical founder can also result in uninformed or wrong-headed thinking about the technical possibilities surrounding your product or service. Unfortunately, consultants tend to be "yes men." Of course they'll agree to do the job—you're essentially paying them to say yes to whatever specs you can dream up! Consultants have a perfectly understandable self interest to minimize pressure or friction while maximizing their billable hours. When the consultant says something can't be done in twenty hours, how can you even argue that it might actually take only two? Getting a consultant's help just isn't the same as having someone on your own team handling the same details. Your project timeline and deliverables will be considerably more suspect when your own team lacks native technical talent. Without a technical cofounder, you simply don't know what you don't know.

GETTING ON THE SAME PAGE

Beyond talking about your idea and all the great things that will come of it, you and your potential cofounders need to be willing to address the points that are often the basis of cofounder conflict. In working through the following checklist, you and your cofounder(s) are likely to see that you can share the same vision, or at least uncover roadblocks that may lie ahead.

- ☑ **Level of cofounder commitment.** In my experience, I've never seen a startup work when the company's founders were not on the scene full-time and 100% committed to the company's growth and success. But if one of your cofounders plans to keep her day job for a while, or if you'll be working part time in a side business, you'll want to know this up front and think through how you'll accommodate the divided commitment.

- ☑ **Non-compete agreements.** Potential founders frequently have a non-compete agreement in place with the company they're leaving. Laws vary from state to state, but at minimum you should make sure that your cofounder is not bound by any such agreements and hence is legally able to work in the industry and geographic location of your startup. Obviously all founders should be willing to sign non-compete agreements for the new startup.

☑ **Pay structure.** The conversation about how you'll each get paid can be tricky, but it's an important one to have. The appetite for risk is relative when it comes to salaries. A married founder with a family may be much more risk-averse than a single person just out of college. The founder who can get by on less today may be willing to defer pay until some specific threshold in the business's growth is reached. If you're bootstrapping, neither of you is likely to get what you're worth, but high founder salaries are not a good place to burn cash anyway. Some investors, like early Facebook investor Peter Thiel, even see low CEO pay as the best predictor of startup success.[18]

☑ **Management and role decisions.** The roles you will each play in the company may seem obvious once you've found your complements, but startup founders often play multiple roles in the beginning, and each of you may be involved to some extent with strategy, sales, legal issues, and finances. It's important to know who will be ultimately responsible for management decisions in these key areas. Be open and honest about the primary activities you each expect to engage in, as well as the tasks you'd rather avoid.

☑ **Intellectual property.** If there are any assets of value in a startup, they are usually in the form of intellectual property—the patents, software, trademarks, designs, or formulas—that will be vital to your business. Before you consummate a startup, you should ask everybody involved about their previous intellectual property history. It's critical that each founder contribute to the company any intellectual property that s/he developed prior to the startup's formation, and everyone should be aware that the company has clear rights and control over intellectual property that will be developed in the future. Partners should be willing to assign technology to the company and to sign non-disclosure agreements for intellectual property either prior to, or at the time of, incorporation.

☑ **Firing and termination.** While this may seem an overly pessimistic subject to be thinking about when you're just starting a company, it's an important one, so the termination conversation needs to take place early on. Donald Trump makes it look easy on television, but that's not the reality for the rest of us. You need to know from the outset how you're going to treat this inevitable situation, so you should all discuss it when heads are cool. If you won't have a Board of Directors, the buck usually stops with the CEO.

☑ **Equity distribution.** This easiest solution to the problem of equity distribution—identical equity splits—is usually not the best. It's rare, if not impossible, for each founder to bring identical value to the table. One founder may have ten more years of experience than the others. He may already have been successful with another startup, or might have far better connections to potential customers or investors. The issue of equity allocation and timing can be extremely difficult for founders to sort out, but it is well worth the effort to think, talk, and debate your way through it.

☑ **Vesting schedule.** Vesting arrangements are the "golden handcuffs" that reinforce founders' loyalty and endurance. There are many ways to handle vesting and to mark the point when the equity becomes yours. Vesting schedules may cover a set period of time; a typical arrangement might be 25% up front and the rest quarterly over a period of four years. There is often a *cliff,* or period of time in which there is no vesting at all, usually six months to a year in the case of founder equity. At the conclusion of this period, known as the *cliff date*, a large amount of vesting occurs all at once. Some arrangements provide for accelerated vesting, in which the vesting is triggered by a specific event such as a change in leadership or some other company milestone. Every member of a company's founding team should be subject to vesting. Most VCs insist on requiring it for founders in early-stage investments.

☑ **Personal goals.** At the very foundation of your working relationship with other founders lie the unique personal and financial goals each of you will be bringing to work every day. If one of you is privately hoping to build a sustainable lifestyle business from which he'll retire after bringing the kids on board, while the other is envisioning a high-growth enterprise with a cashout, you'll both be approaching every group decision from very different angles. If your founder relationship will be a long-term alliance, or at least a long-term friendship, you need to know each other's personal aspirations and goals—what you each expect to achieve and hope to get out of the business.

This will save you plenty of conflict and headaches down the road. The fundamentals of this discussion, and the mutual decisions that evolve from it, can serve as the basis of your Founder's Agreement, a simple written document that will protect everyone's interests and ensure that you all share an understanding from the outset.

ROUNDING OUT THE TEAM

There are many different ideas about what a perfect startup team should look like. In their insightful book, *The Beermat Entrepreneur*, Mike Southon and Chris West propose a very specific list for the ideal makeup of a well-rounded team:[19]

- The entrepreneur
- The technical innovator
- The delivery specialist

- The sales specialist
- The financier

It's a no-brainer that bringing together folks with a wide range of experience will significantly benefit your company. Homogenous teams often result in stale group-think, especially if Patrick Lencioni's concept of "Death by Meeting"[20] isn't incorporated into the culture. Fostering an atmosphere of healthy debate will do more for your startup in the long run than any strict regimen of meetings ever could. In my own personal experience, as well as that of many other entrepreneurs, having a team comprised of people with different perspectives, backgrounds, and skills only helps to strengthen the startup.

Making sure you've got a variety of opinions and skill sets is all well and good, but what about the actual personal attributes of your team members, such as age or management style? Some experts and VCs argue that it's also important to have a variety of personality types on board, while others maintain that a mix of different ages is one of the most crucial components of a robust startup, particularly for attracting venture capital down the road. This is because young people typically contribute passion and creativity, whereas more experienced folks will bring necessary skills and know-how. According to Heidi Roizen, Managing Director for Mobius Venture Capital, having a balanced team composed of eager youngsters and wiser veterans makes VC firms far less likely to typecast your startup as either too vulnerable to rookie mistakes or stuck in a rut with outdated thinking. In his coverage of Roizin's talk, Chris Morris of *Venture Beat* captures it perfectly in his title: "The perfect startup team? Grey hair and mohawks."[21]

I'm not one of these people who tells startups that they should go out and hire the most senior people that they can find. I believe that you should always hire people who are looking to, as Mark Suster puts it, "punch above their weight class"—that is, folks who want to be one league above where they are today. For me, personality and potential often trump experience. But don't confuse potential with the quality of the individual or the skills they can bring to the business. Whether it comes from senior pros or geeky rookies, from working founders or from those who are hired for executive management positions, a good startup team needs to have certain core competencies. A good way to conceptualize this composition is by referring to what I'll call a triangularity of talents.

The Talent Triangle

While working for Ernst & Young's Venture Capital Group, now-independent VC consultant Sean Wise conducted a survey of 500 of the most successful high-growth companies to find out what made for a well-rounded management team. Wise's findings revealed that the most successful management teams included three key attributes:

- **Business acumen** – This person has the skills, knowledge, and experience necessary to make key business decisions.

- **Operational experience** – This is the person who has experience in technical product development, setting up supply chains, inventory management, managing outsourced partners, and other aspects of business

BUSINESS ACUMEN

OPERATIONAL EXPERIENCE   **DOMAIN KNOWLEDGE**

operations.

- **Domain knowledge** – This is the person with a solid understanding of the industry and, perhaps more crucially, the one who is well-connected to a broad network of contacts (who could become potential target customers).

While the survey shows that all three elements of what Wise has dubbed the "Talent Triangle" must be present in an ideally balanced management team with the highest probability of success, Wise also notes that in most cases you don't really need three individuals. What's most important is that the talent components are there, and that they can interact with each other successfully.[22]

Ex-Officio Team Members

Some of your startup team will likely be *ex-officio* members—paid professionals like lawyers, accountants, engineers, or consultants. These people might not be quite as passionate about your startup as you are, but you'll need to have the same degree of trust and confidence in them that you do in your cofounders. You'll be paying these professionals and should be cultivating a long-term working relationship with them, so it's important that they understand your business and your vision. An attorney who has experience with startups, for example, will understand your urgency and be able to expedite the time-consuming agreements and drafting of typical early-stage documents like articles of incorporation or bylaws. He or she will also help you make the decision about what legal form your company should take.

While cash-strapped startups frequently compensate hired professionals by granting them equity in the company, I'm wary of using anything but a miniscule (<1%) amount of equity to pay consultants, service providers, or anyone in an advisory capacity in the early stages of a business. In my opinion, novice cofounders are prone to give too much equity away too quickly. Under the theory that 2% of nothing is still nothing, it can feel like you're getting valuable goods or services for free. But if your business is successful—that *is* the plan, after all, isn't it?—these giveaways can really come back to haunt you. If you find that you need to take this path, try to create a performance-based arrangement. Your company's equity shouldn't be vested until *after* you get the code and the services (legal, accounting, or otherwise) that you need.

FINDING GOOD PEOPLE

The early stages of a startup usually prove to be a busy and chaotic time, and to make matters even more complicated, many of the business structures and processes that will guide you later are not yet in place. For example, you probably won't yet have an official HR department, much less any formal written policies, but you still need to hire in order to grow. You'll likely need to get technical personnel on board quickly, and you'll be eager to fill that key management position that completes the "Talent Triangle" discussed in the previous section.

Here are some ideas on how to prepare for and simplify the hiring process:

- **Decide what sorts of candidates you want to attract.** Come up with some simple bullet points listing the types of characteristics that you're looking for in the ideal candidate and then include those in the actual job posting (e.g., good-natured, professional, self-starting).

- **Identify some easy ways to filter resumes.** One method might be to simply eliminate the resumes of those candidates who were not professional enough to include a personalized cover letter of at least one paragraph.

- **Do phone interviews first, followed up by in-person interviews.** If you're interviewing candidates for a management position that requires significant experience, I strongly recommend that you include the Topgrading techniques outlined in Bradford Smart's exceptional book.[23]

- **Include a written portion in your interview process.** At my company, we use a series of research questions that are not easily answered without effort. This technique helps us evaluate candidates' writing skills, logical thinking, and attention to detail.

- **Consider including a technical assignment where appropriate.** Because we're a SaaS company, it's easy for us to provide a few simple assignments on our web-based application for candidates to complete. This helps us better understand how quickly candidates pick up new technologies and also tells us something about their resourcefulness and their likelihood of success in the company.

I recommend using a variety of different techniques to assess candidates, but remember that there are certain questions that you are legally prohibited from asking—those pertaining to disabilities, marital status, sexual preference, and age, to mention just a few. Before getting involved in the process, interviewers should have a working knowledge of the Equal Employment Opportunity Commission (EEOC) guidelines.[24]

Hiring Outside the Box

Of course, every company is different, but I personally have had great success recruiting heavily from two groups that many companies shy away from when hiring: recent college graduates and experienced part-timers. These two types of hires have added significant value for us.

Recent College Graduates

Many companies are leery of hiring recent college grads as they have little or no track record, require considerable training, and might not work out in the end. But recent college grads tend to be more web-savvy, are active users of social media, and on average are far more energetic and enthusiastic than more seasoned workers. They might be a little wet behind the ears, but the bottom line is that they're eager to learn and to prove themselves.

Here are some pointers based on how our hiring team identifies recent college grads who will do a great job and fit in with our corporate culture:

- **Look for evidence of a strong work ethic.** This might be demonstrated by a high grade point average, a challenging extracurricular activity like a varsity sport, or a full-time job. Sticking with demanding pursuits and being able to balance responsibilities are beneficial traits that will carry over to the workplace.

- **Look for professional and personality traits that fit your organization.** One of my favorite post-interview gestures is receiving a handwritten thank you note in the mail. Ask yourself if this is the sort of person who will get along with coworkers and contribute to the team.

- **Ask extensive personal questions.** You might cover topics such as the person who influenced them the most (aside from their parents), their siblings and their family environment growing up, whether they played sports or music in high school, and so on. These questions might seem irrelevant for a job interview, but the way the candidate answers them will give you insight into their personality and values.

- **Present a career path whenever possible.** This will give candidates an idea of how they can grow in your company, and you can further engage them on this topic to get a better idea of how serious they are about sticking around for a while.

Interviewing is particularly challenging for recent grads or for any entry-level candidate where there's a lack of experience to draw from. It is in these situations where interviewing for personality and values is extremely important. To get the best possible idea as to whether a candidate is compatible with our company culture, we like to arrange significant employee interaction during the interview process. We have as many team members as possible interview the candidate, with the simple message that if any interviewer says no, or has any doubts at all, the candidate is removed from further consideration. Employee consensus is a strong predictive indicator of whether a candidate will be successful if hired. We have very low turnover, and I attribute this in part to the fact that we place so much emphasis on employee consensus in our hiring decisions.

Experienced Part-Timers

A startup that is short on staff and low on cash should be open to hiring experienced part-timers to fill some of its operational needs. Retirees, grad students, parents with school-aged children, or any skilled person who wants to work part-time can add value, even if they're only working for a few hours a day or a couple days a week. The business may not really need a full-time marketing director or HR person, but you can get these duties taken care of by establishing a mutually beneficial relationship with part-time employees. Over time, experienced part-timers can make significant contributions to the growth of the company.

Personality Tests in Startups

As part of a recent Entrepreneurs' Organization forum, we decided to take personality and values tests to learn how we can better relate to the other members of our group. We had the great pleasure of being facilitated and tested by Billy Mullins of Vikus Corporation. The process and outcome really opened my eyes to the benefits of these tests for several reasons:

- Existing team members can gain a better understanding of how they relate to and work with other team members.

- Department teams can identify characteristics missing from their own group and then strive to recruit the personality types that will best fill the gaps and bring certain strengths into the equation.

- Assessments like the Hartman Value Profile are complementary to personality tests like the Myers-Briggs Type Indicator. Analyzing results from several tests will provide a well-rounded profile, helping employees to address areas like work ethic, cooperative nature, and ability to utilize new information.

Based on the positive and rewarding experience I had with

personality testing, my company is now administering tests to existing employees as well as to late-stage job candidates. In addition to the Myers-Briggs and the Hartman Values tests, other possibilities include Calipers and DISC assessments. For startups, especially ones with multiple cofounders, I'd recommend taking some of these tests and looking at the outcome as part of improving your employees' effectiveness. Assembling a harmonious staff is critical in all stages of a business, but it is absolutely fundamental that you put together a well-balanced core of cofounders and team members in the earliest phases of your startup.

CHAPTER 5 ▪ CHOOSING A LOCATION

With the onset of the internet age, some of the conventional business fundamentals of yesteryear have greatly diminished in importance. Essential jobs have been outsourced, many tasks are now automated, and communication has been revolutionized to be both instant and constant. But even with the rise of telecommuting and the virtual office, there's one thing that's still key: location, location, location.

Location is always up there in the top three on those "Why Businesses Fail" lists. Depending on the nature of a new startup, its physical location can very well mean the difference between success and failure. As commercial lease consultant Dale Willerton has pointed out, a good business in a poor location is actually (or will soon become) a poor business.[25] If the company is a brick-and-mortar business, a good location is essential, so considerations like zoning requirements, demographics, traffic patterns, and other competing establishments will be critical. As much as the internet makes searching for commercial real estate easier than ever before, it always helps to seek guidance from a qualified real estate professional, preferably one who understands the target customers and market.

Your own startup might not be as dependent upon location as most retail or consumer services businesses are, but location will still be a consideration for your own well-being and your company's ongoing health. For example, certain parts of the world provide a better business climate for specific types of businesses than other regions.

Back in early 2003, a few years after I'd started my first company, I started doubting myself, questioning the amount of progress we'd made. I had two full-time employees supplemented with a couple of interns, and I just wasn't satisfied with the speed at which things were progressing. Revenues were increasing steadily on a percentage basis, but on an absolute basis they were still pretty meager. I didn't know how to push the ship forward faster without securing outside capital, and after talking to many local angels and VCs, I knew I wasn't going to be able to raise any money because I didn't have a successful startup under my belt and we were competing in a crowded market. Deeply frustrated and unsure of how to proceed, I heard the startup's siren call: *Move to*

California and everything will be better! In California, I'd be able to raise a ton of money, hire an army of great people, and build the next salesforce.com. It was a standard playbook that has been implemented many times before, often with great success. But mentioning California to my change-averse wife-to-be did not go well at all. I didn't know what to do.

After giving it some serious thought while continuing to plug away at my business, I began to realize that I was already in the best place possible for me and for my company. Here are the reasons I made the decision to stay put in Atlanta:

- My friendships and community connections were established and comfortable, and my extended family was in north Florida where I grew up, less than five hours away. This was a big selling point, considering that I'd be starting a family of my own before too long.

- Cost of living had become very important to me. In Atlanta, costs such as housing, food, energy, and entertainment are dramatically lower than in most other metropolitan areas of comparable size.

- I knew that I needed ongoing access to smart young professionals for building out my team. I had recently read several high-profile reports on the growing pool of talent in Atlanta, detailing how successful the city has been in attracting young, educated professionals who are excited about the future and are looking to establish their adult lives somewhere with potential. In addition, Emory, Georgia Tech, and Georgia State continue turn out a steady flow of capable graduates, making the task of hiring quality people much easier.

- Because Atlanta is a regional airline hub, it always has an abundance of direct flights to and from key destinations all over the country. Without this advantage on our side, I knew that sales and travel costs for business development would be higher, and that potential partners and investors might be more reluctant to get involved or to get together.

- I had decided to continue bootstrapping and knew that I wouldn't need to raise money. Atlanta has plenty of angel investors, but there aren't too many venture capitalists around. The next Google-like behemoth is unlikely to come from Atlanta, but plenty of successful and profitable technology companies will. For this reason (among others), Atlanta is a mecca for small and mid-sized technology companies.

Incredibly, the startup's siren call of California is as strong today as it's ever been, based on discussions I've had. But in hindsight, I'm glad I stayed in Atlanta. Little did I know at the time, but we were right on the cusp of explosive growth, and Atlanta has consequently proved to be a great place to build a multi-million-dollar business.

LOCATION, LOCATION, LOCATION!

The advantages of staying at home are hard to overestimate, but if you're considering relocation for your company, it's important to do your homework before making a decision. You can start by taking a look at reputable surveys and rankings. The Small Business Survival Index ranks the fifty U.S. states on how friendly they are to small businesses, but keep in mind that the cost of living, rents, tax structure, licensing fees, and other costs can vary widely by city, even within the same state.[26] *Forbes* magazine also publishes an annual "Best States" ranking, measuring six vital indicators for businesses: costs, labor supply, regulatory environment, current economic climate, growth prospects, and quality of life.[27] *CNN Money* recently profiled eight cities that are offering some pretty attractive perks and incentives to lure new businesses.[28] The Tax Foundation, an online taxpayer resource, produces an annual State Business Tax Index.[29] State and local chambers of commerce are in the business of courting companies to relocate in their respective cities and will be more than happy to provide you with any data you request. The most valuable information, however, will always come from conversations you have with other business owners in the areas you're investigating.

The assumption in most relocation discussions is that businesses will always want to go where the market is bigger, broader, or hotter. As I see it, there are two flaws in this way of thinking. The first error is the failure to take into consideration that the economic profile of a state or city can change rapidly, especially in uncertain economic times like these. This year's "hot" market could well be next year's cold one. Witness the movement in the *Forbes* list over the past few years and you'll have your evidence.

The second error is the blanket assumption that big markets are always best. Depending on your type of business, the smaller or less metropolitan market might actually mean greater profits and fewer headaches for you in the long run. Larger markets are more competitive, and labor and other costs are expensive. The cheaper labor and lower cost of living, along with the accompanying lifestyle advantages (like losing that two-hour daily commute), afforded by locating in a smaller market could turn the market size bias on its head.

At the end of the day, your relocation decision should also take into account how you envision your company developing in the future and the extent to which you want to participate in or influence the industry or community on a local or regional level. For me, headquartering in Georgia meant that I could be a big fish in a small pond—an outcome that was preferable to being a small fish in the technology startup ocean that is Silicon Valley. All things considered, I felt I was better suited for a small pond where I could have more of an impact. Looking back, I know I made the right decision.

OFFICE SPACE: THE $64,000 QUESTION

There's more than enough material for an entire book dedicated to billion-dollar businesses that were launched out of people's garages. Bill Hewlett and Dave Packard started their company out of what is now affectionately known as the "HP Garage" in Palo Alto, California.[30] A generation later, in nearby Los Altos, two guys named Steve founded the garage-headquartered startup that would become the company we now know as Apple.[31] In 1984, Cisco was launched by a husband-wife team out of their own modest Menlo Park garage, followed in 1988 by Linksys—also out of a garage, this time in Irvine, CA—a company that Cisco would later acquire. And Google, the penultimate ideal for any web-based startup, had its humble beginnings in a Menlo Park, CA garage space that founders Larry Page and Sergey Brin had rented from Susan Wojcicki.[32] So don't feel bad if you're confined to your garage, your basement, or even one end of your kitchen table. If the garage is good enough for these industry titans, it's good enough for your startup. Rest assured that, sooner or later, you'll be moving up to classier digs.

Trying to find the right office space often presents a challenge: *How do you get the biggest, best space for the least amount of money?* This is the $64,000 question. I don't have all the answers, but here are some of my pointers for space hunting.

"While you don't always get what you pay for in leasing commercial space, you don't normally get more than you pay for either."

— **Dale Willerton**

➢ *Zoning*

Zoning requirements should be investigated early on in your search. The last thing you want to do is commit to a location where you're legally prohibited from doing business. Make sure that you're looking at commercial-zoned properties if you intend to operate a company out of the chosen location.

➢ **Labor and Talent**

Make sure you set up shop in an area where you have access to the type of labor you require. For instance, if you run a technology firm, consider locating in an area with other high-tech businesses so you can tap into a qualified labor pool. Areas with several colleges, universities, or training institutes also provide a great source of talented, skilled potential employees.

➢ **Structure and Systems**

Before signing a lease agreement, ask some important questions about the condition of the space you're considering. How old is the building? Are its plumbing, heat and A/C, and electrical systems up to code? Can its infrastructure handle your technological needs?

➢ **Convenience**

Once you've narrowed your choices down to several locations, explore the surrounding area of each thoroughly enough to be able to analyze the pros and cons of that location. You want to consider things like the proximity of your business to transit options and airports, nearby hotels and convention centers (if applicable), restaurants and shopping, and any vendors that provide goods or services that your business will require on a regular basis. Our office is located right on the MARTA line (Atlanta's rapid transit entity), and this has been extremely convenient, not only for employees who appreciate having an additional commute option, but also for visitors who can hop on the train and go directly from the airport to our office building.

➢ *Insurance*

Check with your insurance provider regarding what coverage will cost at your new location. Insurance quotes can vary widely depending on location, and high quotes frequently imply that the area in question has particularly high-crime areas, poor police and fire response rates, or some other significant safety and security concern. Not only will you know what your new costs might be in that location, but you'll also be tipped off to locations you might want to avoid.

➢ *Image*

Your space has to work for you, your employees, your customers, and future investors. If your location is in a run-down neighborhood, that can send a negative message, especially to potential recruits. If your building is poorly maintained or half-empty, you and your team will likely suffer, and so will your company's reputation. Your location and office space should ideally reflect who you are as a company, so keep image in mind when selecting your space.

The items I mentioned above are all things that people often forget to consider when looking for the best deal on office space. They might seem like minor points now, but in hindsight, you will be glad that you took them into consideration when choosing your location.

TO LEASE OR TO SUBLEASE?

Once you've settled on your space, you'll want to get legal advice to assist you in negotiating a favorable lease agreement and to help you understand the fine print. Commercial leases are written to benefit the landlord or owner, *not* a young cash-strapped startup, so sometimes what the lease *doesn't* say can be just as important as what it does say. Your attorney should be able to decode most of the obscure legalese for you during the negotiations process. For example, if your lease includes provisions for "miscellaneous expenses," be sure you understand exactly what that means by asking for an explicit list of covered and excluded expenses. Get clarity on who pays for janitorial service and utilities; the same goes for maintenance and landscaping of common areas. Find out what happens if your building is sold to someone else during your lease term (an especially important precaution to take in light of the recent foreclosure crisis), and confirm that your lease contains clear language in regard to build-outs and non-disturbance clauses. If anything is left in doubt, have it spelled out explicitly. And always be sure, as the old saying goes, to *get it in writing*.

For the startup personality, the impulse here is to cut corners and do it yourself. You might save a few bucks in the short term, but this could turn out to be a costly mistake. You'll be much better off in the long run paying a conscientious attorney instead of letting a word or phrase in your office lease negatively affect your earnings for years or force you to unexpectedly alter your business model.

One of the most fundamental questions you need to ask yourself is whether leasing or subleasing is a better option for your growing company. Over the past ten years, I've signed one direct lease and four subleases for office space. Needless to say, we typically relocated every couple of years as we inevitably grew out of our space. It wasn't until the last two subleases that I discovered a very valuable and effective negotiating strategy. This is the number one tip I want all entrepreneurs to know before attempting to negotiate a lease or sublease: *Ask to pay for only the space you need now and grow into the space financially by paying for more over the life of the lease.*

When you're looking for office space for your startup, I'd recommend getting the amount of space you expect you'll need during the last 6-12 months of the lease. For example, you might have five employees now, and you're signing a three-year lease;

you expect you might have about 20 employees by the time the lease is up, so plan accordingly and look for an appropriate amount of space. This seems to be a simple enough calculation, but things can get tricky when your company grows quickly or unexpectedly. It can be tough to estimate your company's potential growth, especially in the early stages of a startup—you're essentially trying to predict the future. You don't want to underestimate and grow out of your leased space prematurely, but you also don't want to pay extra when you overestimate and growth is slower than expected. This conundrum can best be addressed by following the strategy of growing into your leased space. Here's an quick scenario that will illustrate what I mean by "growing into" an office space:

1. Let's say you find 5,000 sq ft of suitable office space, but you don't currently need that much space and you also can't afford the total monthly rent.

2. You only need 1,500 sq ft of space, and you can afford that amount of space at a discounted rate of $18 per foot per year, for a three-year lease term.

3. In your lease negotiations, offer to rent 1,500 sq ft of the available space for the first six months of the three-year lease, followed by 2,500 sq ft the next six months, and add another 1,000 sq ft to the bill every six months thereafter until you're paying for the entire 5,000 sq ft space.

4. The $18/ft/yr rate would stay constant or increase 3% per year so that that by the end of the lease you're paying the standard asking price.

Naturally, your effective rate per square foot over the life of the lease will be significantly less than $18 per square foot, but you'll get the benefit of the space you're going to need at a price that matches your company's growth. This lets you avoid the situation of underestimating your size needs and prematurely outgrowing your office space, or worse, overestimating them and getting locked into a lease you can't afford.

Aside from the golden tip I shared above, I'm also a big advocate of subleasing spaces. I've discovered that you can consistently rent office space for as little as 50% of the market rate using these and similar approaches during normal market conditions, and possibly even less during high-vacancy periods in which you have more negotiating power. Landlords generally like to develop relationships with growing companies and enjoy seeing startups succeed, so this is often a good option to pursue.

CHAPTER 6 ■
LET'S GET STARTED

When people ask me to describe the ideal startup process, I invariably give them what I think is the only truthful answer: *There isn't one*. Every startup is unique, and it's no more possible to describe the ideal startup process than it is to describe the ideal snowflake. Startups shouldn't be viewed as having to follow a certain formula for success. There is no one-size-fits-all manual. There's no tidy enumerated checklist through which you can confidently work your way, ticking off tasks and milestones as though they were step-by-step IKEA assembly instructions. Because everybody's tasks and milestones will be different, I can't provide that checklist. What I *can* do is describe the general progression through which all startups move, as well as a cluster of activities and decisions that I think have to be made early on in order to set your startup on the path to success.

The concept stage of a startup, also called the "napkin stage," is the formative phase during which your idea begins to gel. What started as merely a few scribbles on a cocktail napkin has begun to take shape. The concept stage usually lasts for anywhere from three to six months, at which point the concept either is abandoned or advances to the seed stage. All startups go through this stage, some of them faster than others.

If you've answered most of the big questions about how you're going to make your vision happen, and if you've been fortunate enough to have found suitable cofounders who can come to agreement on equity distribution and the more significant management issues, you've already made many pivotal decisions and done most of the heavy lifting associated with the concept stage. There are other decision points, however, that surface early on; these critical junctures require choices to be made sooner rather than later. I have outlined some of the most important of these below.

WHAT'S IN A NAME?

Among the earliest considerations faced by a new startup will be what to call the business. This decision involves selecting the names that will identify your business legally and to your market. Because today almost every business will in some way be an e-business, I believe that the domain name should be nailed down first.

Domain Name

A good domain name is important for any company today, but for a software company or web-based business, it's absolutely essential. The challenge, however, is that it is difficult (and often expensive) to find a good name that isn't already taken. Here are some rules I try to follow:

- The domain name should be 10 characters or less.
- It must be a dot-com domain and not a secondary extension (.biz, .info, .net, etc.).
- It should be phonetically spelled and easily spoken in English.
- It should always be purchased—*not* rented or leased—from someone else.
- It should not be easily confused with the name of a competitor or any related businesses.
- Ideally it will be relevant to the business (but read on to see why this is optional).
- It should not already be trademarked.

To meet these requirements, I've generally found it takes a

budget of $500-$2,000 and the purchase of an existing domain on Sedo.com (a domain marketplace). It is still worth trying sites like BustAName.com, Register.com, GoDaddy, and Network Solutions to find an unregistered domain, but I haven't had luck going that route for a while now. If your search for obvious and relevant names leads only to frustration, it's possible to get really creative, even to "invent" a name as new as the business you're beginning.

Back in 2006, I had started to develop marketing software that would help with lead generation and management. I didn't own any suitable domain names at the time, so I set out in search of a new domain name that would serve as the basis for the company name. After using several domain name-finding tools and not having any luck, on a lark I went to Dictionary.com and typed in "marketing." (At the time, Dictionary.com returned translations of a word in 29 different languages.) Nothing useful turned up for "marketing," so I did a search for "market." Of the translations that came back, one caught my eye: *pardot*. Pardot is the Latvian verb meaning "to market" or "to sell." I liked that the word was easy to pronounce and spell, so I headed over to BustAName to see if it was unregistered, and sure enough, it was available. I registered it immediately for eight bucks, and since then Pardot has grown to become an eight-figure revenue business.

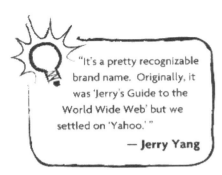

"It's a pretty recognizable brand name. Originally, it was 'Jerry's Guide to the World Wide Web' but we settled on 'Yahoo.'"

— **Jerry Yang**

Don't despair if your preferred choices are already taken. Just keep thinking and you're bound to come up with something good. A great name is one of the best marketing tools you'll ever have, and it has become increasingly more valuable with the rise of social media and word-of-mouth advertising. Unique names are especially useful, and if your domain and business name is short and memorable, it may not even have to mean anything—at least not yet. After all, who had ever heard of a "Coke" before 1886, or a "Band-Aid" before the advent of that product? And how about "Google" for a business name?

Like the decision about whether or not you should secure a less-than-desirable dot-biz or dot-net domain, it is also a tough call as to whether or not you should register domain names that are obvious typos, alternate spellings and sound-alikes. Your decisions will likely be dependent on what your budget is and how important search engine marketing will be to your business.

However, I have one minor warning when it comes to domain names. Many people frequently purchase and register their domain names through the web hosting service that will host their website. When you do this, the domain name belongs to you, and in the event you change services, you should in theory be able to move it easily. But the reality is that it is not unheard of for a less-than-scrupulous hosting company to make it very difficult to wrest your domain name away from them. I recommend registering yourself through a domain name registrar, an extra but essential step that ensures that you are registered as the owner as well as the administrative and technical contacts.

Business Name

Ideally, your business name and domain name will be identical or at least similar, but again, I'd strongly suggest giving priority to the selection of your domain name. Securing the legal rights to a business name depends on the legal structure of your business, but only technically speaking. If you plan to have a sole proprietorship, your business will be registered and licensed through your local county business office. A corporation, on the other hand, will have to be searched, cleared, and recorded through your Secretary of State's website. But regardless of which of these approaches you take neither one will protect you or secure your name for interstate commerce or international trade, nor will it guarantee that you won't be infringing on someone else's trademark rights. The only way you can be assured of real protection is by doing a thorough nationwide search, starting with both registered and common law (unregistered) trademarks, both of which provide federal protection through the United States Patent and Trademark Office.

You can "do business as" something other than the name of your sole proprietorship, partnership, or corporation by filing for DBA status. *DBA* or *d/b/a* is a legal term that simply indicates that the name under which a business is operating to the public is not actually the same name as the legal entity or individual who owns and is responsible for it. This is sometimes referred to as a "fictitious" name, in that the fictitious name does not reveal the identity for the person or entity who is actually legally responsible for the business. It might not be necessary for everyone, but where it is applicable, this method allows you to shorten your operating name, which in many cases can be a smart move. For example, my actual business name could be something long and unwieldy like "Virtual Accounting Services USA, LLC," but provided the *d/b/a* designation is used, it can be referred to simply as "Virtual Accounting." Imagine how much nicer that looks on websites, signage, and other marketing materials.

One final word of advice on registering your business name and domain: There may be reasons why you need to use your home address at first, but keep in mind that once your business name and domain name are registered, all of the recorded contact information, including business address and telephone numbers, become available to the public.

Usernames

Another simple piece of advice for entrepreneurs is to immediately reserve their chosen company name as a username on popular services like Twitter, Facebook, and LinkedIn. The username has to be unique to the service and acts much like a domain name where it is issued on a first-come, first-served basis. Registering the name early on doesn't cost anything, so reserving it is a good move even if you don't have plans to use it immediately. I typically recommend starting with usernamecheck.com, a site that helps streamline the process of reserving your company's username.

IT'S ALL LEGALESE TO ME

The type of business entity your company will be, and the ownership structure it will have, are things that must be determined before you can acquire even the most basic documents and operational tools—business licenses, federal tax ID numbers, and so on—that you will need to conduct business. By incorporating, your startup can take advantage of certain tax filing options and personal risk protections that you would otherwise be missing. Which legal structure you choose—whether it's an LLC, an S-Corp, or a C-Corp—will depend on the specifics of your business. Which state you incorporate in may be dictated by industry standards or legal restrictions, or it may be left up to you to decide.

A company might choose to incorporate as a *C-Corporation* (C-Corp) if it is looking to raise money. C-Corps pay taxes on corporate profits and then shareholders are taxed only on dividends, not the company's profits as a whole, making this an attractive arrangement for potential investors who don't want to amass more tax documents each year. Because C-Corps are more flexible than S-Corps, they are well suited to large companies with lots of shareholders, particularly a publicly traded company. An *S-Corporation* (S-Corp) has stricter requirements, in that it only allows one class of stock, but its primary advantage is that it provides tax benefits for companies looking to avoid double taxation (as is the case with a C-Corp). If the potential tax benefits become significant enough to warrant it, a C-Corp may change its status to an S-Corp; reverting back to a C-Corp is also possible, should the company need to do so in the future. A *limited liability company* (LLC) has far fewer formalities to follow, single taxation like an S-Corp, and is comparatively easy to set up, in addition to allowing its members more flexibility with regard to management and ownership arrangements. These benefits make LLCs a popular choice for most startups.

Obviously I'm not a tax advisor or attorney, but I thought an overview of these legal structures might be helpful. Final decisions regarding such matters as which entity is most suitable for your company, or whether to incorporate outside of your home state, should only be made with the help of a qualified legal advisor.

THE BUSINESS PLAN

All of the big-name business gurus, top financial advisors, and even your grad school professor will tell you that you absolutely, positively *must* have a written business plan for any new venture. I disagree. Most startups don't require the level of detail in a conventional business plan, and in most cases, the details that you could provide at such an early stage would be only speculative—hopeful but, frankly, uneducated guesses. Typical business plans can run anywhere from 20 to 50 pages and often take months to prepare. The time, effort, and money invested in creating a business plan is better spent in other arenas—namely, getting your business up and running!

Of course, if you're going after investors, you'll need an executive summary and pitch deck, so you might as well get some pieces of a plan together. It should be well-organized, clearly articulated, and as comprehensive as you can make it. The spelling and grammar does matter, as does your plan's appearance and presentation.

I'd like to take a slightly different approach to the question of a business plan. I've found it most helpful to use the elements of a traditional business plan as springboards for thinking

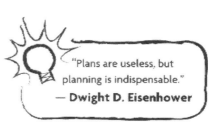

"Plans are useless, but planning is indispensable."
— **Dwight D. Eisenhower**

and planning, for creating a "roadmap" for your company, and for revealing what, even at this early stage, you really should be committing to paper. Let's look at the standard components.

Executive Summary

The first piece of a business plan is the executive summary. It describes who you are, what
you do, what pain or problem you solve, and what you want to achieve. The goal is to create a hook in the reader's mind. When it is well done, the executive summary can stand on its own as an independent document. Even if you don't need a formal business plan with a written executive summary, you'll still need its verbal equivalent: that hard-hitting sales tool known as "the pitch."

The Pitch

The pitch is your first and most powerful sales tool—the clear and succinct description of what
you are and what you do. Later your pitch may be formalized through a video or PowerPoint presentation, but in the beginning, as well as many times throughout the course of your business, you'll still need a stand-up, verbal presentation. You should be able to deliver this "elevator speech" quickly, spontaneously, and fluidly, over and over again and whenever necessary. Make sure you practice your pitch, because once your company launches, you will be delivering it more times than you care to count. Here are some of the key aspects of a good pitch:

- **It's descriptive.** A good pitch should clearly communicate *what* it is that you are building or selling. This is without a doubt *the* most important part of a pitch. You don't know how many pitches I've walked away from without having the faintest idea of what the presenter was actually doing. You don't need to explain everything you're doing in minute detail; most products are far too nuanced to be explained in 30 seconds anyway. You simply need to explain what your product does (or what your service provides) in a way that your audience will understand. Stick to the big picture and you'll be fine.

- **It's compelling.** A good pitch always demonstrates *why* someone would use your product. You need to connect with your audience in a way that shows them why your product is going to be a huge hit. Sometimes this can be tough if your audience isn't the target customer, but in some ways it can be an advantage because you get to define the problem and the solution.

- **It's conversational.** Your pitch should communicate your ideas clearly and in simple conversational terms. You might be tempted to write out your pitch and then read it aloud. Don't do that. A pitch that looks great on paper can sound stiff and unnatural once it's actually spoken. Pretend you are explaining your product to a good friend or colleague by describing it aloud—only then should you think about putting your words on paper (if you must). A video camera can help in this department. Just sit in front of it and explain your product ten different ways. Then watch the recording and note what sounds natural, and what doesn't. Eventually you'll find idioms and phrases that not only sound good, but also communicate your ideas both naturally and economically.

One of the best ways to improve your pitch is to watch other pitches. It doesn't take long before you start to see the difference between good and bad pitches. TechCrunch offers a great resource where you can do just that, as does the site demo.com.

Company Overview

The next section of a business plan contains a description of your business, a brief history of the company, and a list of key members of the leadership team. This part is pretty straightforward and most likely you won't have to write it down. But nevertheless, there are a couple of "springboard" items normally included in this section that should be well thought out, discussed with your team, and committed to paper early on: your company's mission and vision statements.

The Mission Statement

Your mission statement should encapsulate what it is that your company does or wants to accomplish. Your mission statement can be aspirational, but make sure you decide on something that's actually achievable. Branding expert Marty Neumeier, author of *The Brand Gap* and *Zag*, conceptualizes the mission statement as what he calls the "core purpose" of a company—what your company aims to do aside from making money.[33] You will only arrive at an effective mission statement once you've defined your company's unique focus or core purpose and articulated it in a concise declaration of intent.

Mission statements can be simple (e.g., Pepsi's rather blunt "Beat Coke") or ambitious (e.g., Nike's mission to "bring inspiration and innovation to every athlete in the world"). Google has certainly lived up to its straightforward mission to "organize the world's information and make it universally accessible and useful." Intel's mission statement ("to delight our customers, employees, and shareholders by relentlessly delivering the platform and technology advancements that become essential to the way we work and live"), while a little unwieldy, actually manages to capture a lot of key elements in a single sentence. As all of these illustrate, the mission statement should express your company's focus on a worthwhile and achievable goal.

The Vision Statement

If your mission statement is "do-able," your vision statement should be "dream-able." It's really not a statement of a quantitatively achievable goal, but rather an inspirational goal that describes a long-term, idealized scenario of what you would like your company to achieve or to become. Walt Disney's was simply "to make people happy"—not truly achievable in a literal sense, but definitely a great ideal to work toward. At Amazon.com, the vision is to be "earth's most customer-centric company; to build a place where people can come to find and discover anything they might want to buy online." This sounds like somewhat of a long shot until you consider the fact that you can buy pretty much anything on Amazon, and that the customer service is among the best out there. Vision statements can be used internally to motivate employees and management, and they can be used externally to project a certain image of your company and its values.

To recap, your mission statement says what your company is or does, while your vision statement tells what it seeks to achieve or become. These statements should both be brief, powerful, and honest. Even without a formal business plan, your mission and vision statements should comprise a central part of your early startup documents and will quickly become part of your roadmap.

Financial Model

Financial models have a notoriously bad reputation because they are always wrong, but the exercise of creating them has tremendous value. The effort forces you to think critically and to examine the key drivers of your business. So, while the pragmatist in you might be tempted to skip this step with the rationale that everything will work itself out, keep in mind that you will benefit in other ways from the learning experience.

The classic business plan typically contains several financial documents. I've seen this section run 10+ pages of dense tables filled with microscopic metrics. Ultimately you'll have to come up with a balance sheet and a profit and loss statement, but in the very beginning you'll only need a few simple spreadsheets to build a really simple cash flow model that lets you see if the math makes sense. The most important documents to start with are the expense summary and the sales forecast, which together will allow you to complete your "break-even" analysis.

Expense Summary

To create an expense summary, you'll first need to estimate your startup costs and then extend operating expenses across three years. Even after you've thought of everything and been excessively generous with your estimates of expenses, opening your new business is still likely to cost more than initially anticipated. It's a good idea to create a contingency line item to account for the surprise expenses that are sure to come along.

Sales Forecast

Prepare a sales forecast by coming up with a month-by-month projection and putting it in another spreadsheet. Divide your projected monthly sales into whatever components, natural divisions, or obvious categories that might apply to your business. Of course you won't get everything right from the get-go, but arrive at the best educated guesses you can so that you can use these projections later on to see where you guessed wrong.

It's also a good idea to create two forecasts: the "best case scenario" forecast that describes what you'd expect if everything goes as planned, and a "worst case scenario" forecast that estimates the minimum goal that you're confident you can reach. Keep notes on your research and details on any other assumptions that you used to build the sales forecast.

Break-Even Analysis

Now that you've completed your expense summary and sales forecast, you have what you need to perform a "break-even" analysis—a prediction of how much product you'll have to sell, at a given price, to recover your total costs. You now know the dividing line between operating at a loss and operating at a profit. From this simple starting point, you have all the foundations in place upon which you can later base your balance sheets, budgets, profit and loss (P&L) statements, and any other financials you might need.

The truth is that few (if any) business assumptions survive past the first customer. Once you actually start selling things to real people, as opposed to relying on your educated guesses, you'll have hard data with which to form more accurate future projections. Your simplified business plan will either be a living document that continually evolves, or else will sit untouched in its file, nothing more than a testament to your finest experiment in creative writing. Should a bank or other entity request a business plan, you can always prepare a longer conventional one later on, once you've accumulated some real-life experience and learned from some of your mistakes, ensuring that there will be much more education backing up those "educated" guesses. In fact, you may find it useful to set up the outline for your business plan and fill in the details as they become apparent to you. In the meantime, start signing customers and begin learning what it will take to make your business a success.

> "As your company grows, you can grow your planning. Grow it like an artichoke grows, with leaves—more details, more specifics, more description-surrounding the heart."
>
> — **Tim Berry**

Chapter 7 ■
The Importance of
Being Scrappy

Many of us remember the dot-com bubble of the 1990s pretty vividly. The era was marked by an irrational exuberance for the commercial potential of the internet. Web-based companies known as "dot-coms" sprung up by the hundreds on what seemed like a daily basis. Eager venture capitalists fought each other hand over fist simply to win the privilege of providing funding to any one of the endless stream of visionaries touting untested ideas and outlandish concepts. There were absurdly inflated stock valuations for companies that had never made a dime. There were countless college dropouts becoming instant millionaires. Mostly, though, the seemingly endless stream of cash was further fueled by the burning desire to spend it on the next big thing.

There's no shortage of stories about well-capitalized companies that suddenly exploded onto the scene but quickly fizzled out and died. One of the most startling examples I can think of is the British web sensation Boo.com, an online fashion retailer. This particular dot-com launched late in 1999, managed to burn through $135M in venture capital in just 18 months, and, just as quickly as it all started, met an untimely demise when it was placed in receivership in the spring of 2000.[34] In a June 2008 article, CNET dubbed the Boo.com implosion one of the greatest dot-com disasters in history. But while it may rank among the most conspicuous of the dot-com crash-and-burns, the Boo.com debacle was by no means unique. The entire era was characterized by the meteoric rise and subsequent (often swift) collapse of many heavily funded companies that simply burned through their investment capital before ever making a profit.

Ironically, the phenomenal pace at which these dot-coms burned through their initial investment capital helped conceal the fact that many of them amounted to little more than a house of cards in the first place. Shareholders mistook those high burn rates as indications of a fast-growing customer base and continued to invest even in the face of declining stock value. In fact, some financial analysts blame the entire dot-com crash on excessive burn rates and overly optimistic predictions of when positive cash flow could be achieved.

Well, those days are over, and good riddance to them. The kind of reckless abandonment we saw during the heyday of the dot-com boom just doesn't work anymore. Young unprofitable companies with excessive burn rates and overly optimistic forecasts are not admired anymore, and after so many VCs learned tough lessons the hard way, companies like these rarely appeal to investors.

The metrics *burn rate* and *cash zero date* are both venture capital terms that came into vogue during the dot-com era when it was common for a tech startup to go through several rounds of funding before finally reaching positive cash flows. Simply put, your burn rate is how much money you lose each month. It's the speed at which you're going through your cash, and it provides the time measure, or *zero date*, for when you must either make a profit, find additional funding, or go out of business.

The critical measure for startups is knowing what that burn rate is at all times and managing it well. Watching cash flow is even more critical when you don't have deep pockets, so pay close attention. Ideally, entrepreneurs should have a *reserve funding plan*—a financial Plan B for ensuring that your cash flows don't fall below dangerous levels. At the very least you'll want to review your burn rate every month, just as you also monitor the components of the burn-rate equation: *expenses and income*. In times of a cash crunch, you may need to keep closer tabs on your cash flow; in fact, checking it daily is a good idea.

THE CASH CONVERSION CYCLE

A topic related to burn—one that startup founders don't usually think through—is the cash conversion cycle, or in layman's terms, how much work and time it takes to make a sale, deliver the goods or services, and to get paid. At first glance, it might seem like a non-issue. You sell something and you get paid, right? Well, it's not nearly that simple. Let's walk through a typical cash conversion cycle for a product's sales and implementation timeline:

- You start calling on companies to build a sales pipeline for three months.

- You discover that your average sales cycle requires two months. Now you're at five months before the first sale.

- Your policy is to collect 50% up front and 50% upon completion. You bill *net 30 days*, which means your customer has 30 days to pay you.

- It takes 60 days to do the implementation, conduct training, and make sure the client is happy.

- You invoice the client for the final 50%, also net 30 days.

What has transpired in the above scenario is three months of calling, two months of selling, and 30 days of waiting for the check. It has taken six months for your first dollar to come in. Then it has taken two months to implement, and another 30 days to get paid the rest of what you are owed (which is three more months after getting the first partial payment). In this example of a cash conversion cycle, it really takes nine months from launch to get full payment in the till. Obviously, any company following this model must keep a critical and realistic eye on how long it takes cash to move through the business.

In addition to understanding your company's cash conversion cycle, entrepreneurs also need to worry about the management of accounts receivable and customer credit as much as, if not more than, large companies do. (Of course, large companies can be just as guilty of paying slowly as can small cash-strapped or underfinanced startups.) Regardless of the company's size, entrepreneurs need to do normal credit investigations and have a credit approval process in place for their customers. Being aware of the actual payment habits of your customers will help you to have cash on hand when you need it and make your cash budgeting more realistic.

So, aside from monitoring your cash conversion cycle and making sure you have a well-controlled burn rate, what else should you be doing to promote your company's financial security? Above all else, your startup needs to be scrappy. More of a state of mind than an actual strategy, being scrappy entails making the most out of limited resources. Not only will it help you build a lean, mean startup, but it can also bring other unexpected benefits.

THE SCRAPPY STARTUP MINDSET

All startups, bootstrapped or not, should start from Day One with a scrappy mindset. I don't so much mean "scrappy" in the sense of picking fights, although any startup has to have a fighting spirit and must be unafraid to meet challenges head-on. Here I am using this term to indicate a thrifty do-it-yourself (DIY) approach to launching a startup that enables you to do more with less. Conserving your resources whenever you're able allows you to stretch your money further, thereby buying you time to achieve success. That's not to say that every penny must be saved for the sake of proving a point, but rather, wherever possible and logical, you should try to go the cheap and frugal route. Let's look at some ways to be scrappy:

- **Consider subleasing your office space.** Finding an office sublease could save you up to 50% off the market rental rates. A sublease will also enable you to have a shorter lease term, which is a smart move since you can't predict how fast your company will grow or how many employees you'll need in two to three years.

- **Furnish your space on a dime.** Purchase used furniture from office liquidation centers, or look for a local company that is downsizing or going bankrupt. Many of these companies will give you their unwanted furniture for free, because otherwise they'd have to pay to have it removed.

- **Go for refurbished.** Purchase refurbished laptops and monitors directly from the manufacturer (e.g., Apple) or from reputable online discount retailers such as TigerDirect and NewEgg. Never buy these things new— technology is improving constantly, so the premium you pay for new items really isn't worth it. And try to be versatile with your choices; for example, purchase laptops instead of desktops so that employees have mobility and can work in any setting.

- **Buy in bulk, but only when it makes sense.** Take advantage of the "Big Box" stores when you really need quantity, but don't let them make a sucker out of you. It can take a really, really long time to use 100,000 paperclips.

- **Make the most of technology.** Use a VoIP (Voice over Internet Protocol) phone system like Vocalocity or Cbeyond instead of a traditional analog line. These are considerably cheaper and much more feature-rich. But above all, your business must have a dedicated phone line with voicemail, both of which can be obtained through services like Skype and GoogleVoice.

- **Always ask for the discount, price break, or promotional**

offer. If you find that too embarrassing, you're in for a tough time as an entrepreneur. Remember: It never hurts to ask.

- **Every little bit helps.** In Ted Turner's autobiography, he recollects the time when his television station TBS first started to go national. To gain credibility, TBS would often partner with companies running late-night infomercials to do the order fulfillment for those products. Turner noticed that some of the stamps on the envelopes of incoming orders were not marred by a postmark, so he had his employees carefully remove those stamps and reuse them on outgoing company mail. It might sound like an excessive penny-pinching tactic, but who knows how much money TBS saved by doing this? Just remember that when you're trying to be scrappy, every little bit helps.

- **Barter for goods or services.** The Great Recession has revived this antiquated practice. While some businesses are more obviously suitable to bartering than others, if you don't keep bartering possibilities top of mind, you'll miss opportunities to swap your goods or services for others you might need.

- **Work with suppliers for special payment plans and financial breaks.** Those suppliers want you to make it big and to remember who helped it happen. Don't underestimate the willingness of suppliers to cooperate with your fledgling business.

- **Don't outsource tasks when it will cost you more to do**

so. Don't rely entirely on recruiters; *do* hire slowly and carefully, bringing in a recruiter when it makes sense to do so. Rent it, don't own it. Don't even manage it if you can avoid doing so. But watch out for the hidden costs. Those "small" installment payments add up.

- **Pay your bills on time, but don't pay them early.** If you've got 45 days, take 45 days. One exception to this rule is the Plum Card from American Express, which gives you a discount for early payment and imposes no penalty for extended payment.

The Time vs. Money Tradeoff

When I started my first company, I would pinch pennies whenever and wherever I could. I still do. The big difference now is that I've come to realize that many things are better done by paying full price instead of laboring through several different strategies just to save a few dollars. It can be hard at first to make spending decisions where the *time vs. money* tradeoff comes into play. Scrappy entrepreneurs are wary of spending money unnecessarily, but with experience and practice, it becomes much easier to make these judgment calls. Here are a few examples of the *time vs. money* tradeoff in action:

- **Get professional legal help.** There are many do-it-yourself kits available for incorporating a business, but it's well worth paying a lawyer to walk you through the many legal entity issues and tax considerations. This is a tough call to make because legal costs can easily run into the thousands of dollars, but it's money well spent to get everything set up right the first time.

- **Crowdsource your logo design.** Yes, you can probably design your own logo with Photoshop or a free logo generating site, but paying a couple hundred bucks to one of the many excellent outsourcing sites gets a professionally designed logo that shows you're serious about the business. I've used LogoBee for several of my startups and have been pleased with the results (more about that in a moment).

- **Pay a premium for the premium services you need most.** The difference in quality between a business-class cable modem and a dedicated T1 line is dramatic. In my own experience, I've found that paying several times more for high-quality bandwidth and internet access is a worthy investment.

- **In the office environment, it's the little things that count.** Things you might think of as minor niceties, such as larger monitors, ergonomic desk accessories, and brand-name coffee, can really make a big difference in terms of a happy workforce. In fact, the office coffee machine is one place where you should never skimp. It's sure to get lots of use—a caffeinated employee is a productive employee, after

all—so it's worth spending a little more to buy a high-quality machine and good coffee. Try to lease office space with good natural light and air circulation. You'll have to make your own decision about whether to splurge on things like Aeron chairs, but there are some fundamentals of workplace safety and comfort that, as the MasterCard ads say, are simply priceless.

These are just a few of the areas where I've found that it's better to spend the money and save the time. The old saying about having to spend money to make money still rings true. I'll never forget an experience I had that really drove that lesson home for me.

The Business Card Lesson

I'm generally pretty averse to unnecessary dead trees (read: paper) in business, but I don't scrimp on business cards anymore. Back in 2001, about six months after I had started my first company, I was in Durham, NC participating in a workshop at the Council for Entrepreneurial Development (CED). The workshop leader was discussing ways to set goals and milestones for a business. Her goal at the time was to reach a certain level of sales, and she explained how she was going to reward herself with a $60,000 Lexus SC 430 convertible, so she had a picture of it up on her wall as a reminder. The presentation was engaging and she gave plenty of helpful advice, but as it turned out, I would learn my most valuable lesson after class.

I was pretty impressed with the workshop, and when it ended, I eagerly took advantage of the instructor's offer to answer our individual questions as well as to listen to the elevator pitch for our businesses. I dutifully stood in line until finally it was my turn. She asked for my business card and, not thinking much of it, I handed her my DIY card made from a kit at home on my printer. Immediately she held the card up in the air and flicked it with her finger to illustrate how cheap and flimsy it was. I was mortified. It might seem trivial, she explained, but people notice little details like this and make judgments accordingly. I then realized that my homemade business card reflected poorly on my business and me.

I'll never forget that encounter and the important lesson it taught me: Don't overlook the details in presenting yourself and your company to the world. I always tell fledgling entrepreneurs that it's important to begin building your brand and image early on, as these things really count when you're getting a company off the ground. I'd suggest going through a professional but economical web-based service like LogoBee or LogoYes to design a company logo. And, as I can tell you from personal experience, be sure to have high-quality business cards produced by a professional printing company (we've had success using Printing4Less). Image isn't everything, but it definitely counts for something.

BUILDING A SCRAPPY CORPORATE CULTURE

So you're being frugal and doing the DIY thing; this is all well and good until you start hiring employees. How can you make sure they share your scrappy mindset? You can certainly start by trying to hire folks with compatible values, but even individuals who are normally quite frugal in their personal lives can be a little cavalier about spending the company's money. A better bet would be to build a corporate culture that reflects these values. Instilling the scrappy mindset into your employees at the beginning of the business isn't difficult, and it can reap tangible and intangible rewards that far outweigh any effort expended. Here are just a few ideas on how to build a scrappy corporate culture from the get-go:

- **Crowdsource the deals.** Post a list of equipment you're on the lookout for, or supplies you're going to need, in the break room or some other heavy-traffic common area and encourage employees to speak up when they hear about sales or bargains.

- **Make it a game.** There will always be people who genuinely enjoy bargain hunting and coupon clipping. Seek out these employees and put them in charge of getting deals for the company.

- **Unleash the (bargain) hounds.** Encourage everyone on your team to ask, "Is that your best price?" whenever they rent a car, check into a hotel, or buy services or supplies. This simple question can yield surprising results in real cash savings over time and will help to ensure that your employees spend the company's money as if it were their own.

- **Give credit where credit is due.** Recognize employee efforts in cost savings and acknowledge them personally or in emails.

- **Set expectations and lead by example.** Any attempt to build a frugal mentality into the corporate culture will backfire if you and your cofounders hold yourselves to different standards by refusing to use both sides of the paper, insisting on flying first class, or forgetting to turn out the lights when you leave your office. When everyone knows that frugality is expected of every single employee up to the CEO, people will behave accordingly.

Encouraging a scrappy mindset doesn't have to make you come

across as Scrooge. It can actually build team spirit and make everyone feel like you all have your shoulders to the same wheel. Scrappiness also provides a great foundation for corporate culture; if you start out doing something cheaply out of economic necessity, it may become a revered company tradition. I like that the ramen noodles we always stock in our office break room remind me of eating ramen in my dorm room during the early days of my first startup (cheap and fast!). And if, like Jeff Bezos and the employees of the first incarnation of Amazon.com, you build a great company together on repurposed doors that you're using for desks, you'll all have great stories to tell in the future.

CHAPTER 8 ▪ LAUNCHING LEAN: HOW LOW CAN YOU GO?

The rise of the lean startup movement in recent years has everybody talking about launching lean. To give an oversimplified definition, launching lean involves doing as much market development as possible with limited resources. This philosophy could theoretically apply to any company, but it is especially salient among the technology community, where it has become nothing short of a mantra for startups. With so many tools and resources at our disposal, and with the stark realities of limited funding, tech startups really have no excuse to do otherwise. Launching lean not only asks us to trim costs and avoid wasting our resources, but it also requires us to be agile, flexible, and responsive. Just as with a limbo champion, it's not just about how low you can go, but how gracefully and nimbly you do it.

THE LEAN STARTUP MOVEMENT

The slow-burn, cash-frugal approach discussed in the previous chapter is part and parcel of what has become known as the "lean startup" movement. As an entrepreneur myself—one who has learned a lot of lessons the hard way—I've now become a huge proponent of this school of thought. The lean startup movement is not just opposed to wasting cash, but also frowns upon squandering energy, resources, or time in any context. This approach emphasizes shortening the path between your initial product vision and what the customer actually wants.

The term "lean startup" was coined by engineer and serial entrepreneur Eric Ries. Ries drew his inspiration from the Japanese lean manufacturing processes (popularized by Toyota, among other companies), which focused on chiseling away any superfluous work and investment of resources that didn't directly produce value for its customers. The concept can be applied to any business that faces uncertainty about what its customers want, but it is especially applicable to innovative startups.

The lean startup methodology's primary aim is to keep costs low by reducing waste while still remaining as flexible as possible, in order to ship the best possible products in the shortest time possible. The process depends on customer input and constant iteration of new ideas and improvements. Ries identifies three trends that converged within the lean startup movement:

1. Increasing use of open source and free software

2. Adoption of agile development methodologies

3. Iterative customer-driven product development

The obvious benefit of the trend toward using open source and free software is that it makes it possible to build a new product quickly and with little effort due to the re-use and reconfiguration of existing modules. This has made it easier for startups to respond quickly to market demands. The latter two trends also have their own associated benefits, which we'll discuss in more detail below.

Agile Development Methodologies

Agile development is an approach to software development that originated in reaction to traditional engineering methodologies, which were too hung up on rigid requirements and bureaucratic processes. The agile development philosophy prized flexibility and responsiveness over adherence to fixed procedures, with the ultimate intention to reduce waste and unlock creativity in the product development process. Scrum is the most popular and widely used of the agile development methodologies.

The manifesto of The Agile Development Alliance[35] states that this school of thought values:

- Individuals and interactions over processes and tools
- Working software over comprehensive documentation
- Customer collaboration over contract negotiation
- Responding to change over following a plan

It's easy to see why the agile approach is so well-suited to software. Like any technology, software is continuously evolving, perhaps at a faster rate than any other category of consumables. Consequently, customer needs change constantly, and any company that hopes to be competitive will need to become adept at iterating—that is, changing course quickly and unexpectedly in order to respond successfully to changes in the marketplace or new technologies.

Customer-Driven Product Iteration

Agile development recognizes that responding to the market is fundamental to a company's success. It is no surprise, then, that customer-driven product development has also been a cornerstone of the lean startup movement. But it's not enough to simply take customer needs into consideration—you must do it quickly and effectively.

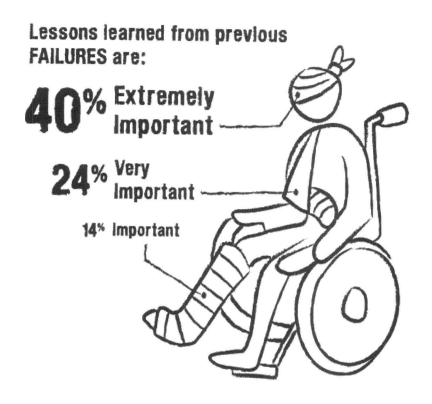

Lessons learned from previous FAILURES are:

40% Extremely Important

24% Very Important

14% Important

From Kauffman Foundation study, *Anatomy of a Successful Entrepreneur* (2009)

Agile product development follows less of the old regimented model of releasing versions periodically and more closely resembles an ongoing process of constant iterations. Ries termed this concept—and I'm quoting verbatim here because I love the adjective he uses—*"ferocious* customer-centric rapid iteration."[36] For me, Ries's descriptive phrasing highlights the fact that lean startup success comes from a confluence of three attributes: (1) it's aggressively responsive, (2) it's customer-driven, and (3) it's iterative, which means that it will revise and reinvent itself whenever necessary, in a fast, customer-driven process. Wash, rinse, repeat.

I didn't always understand this confluence of factors. As you will see, a great deal of what I've now come to appreciate about the lean startup movement was learned the hard way.

POST-MORTEM OF A FAILED PRODUCT

At the beginning of 2008, I put together a team to build a web content management system (CMS) with community functionality infused throughout. The prototype attempted to incorporate emerging trends such as crowdsourcing and social networking into a traditional CMS. The idea was that companies needed a content management solution that could also facilitate product forums, customer communities, idea exchanges, wikis, and blogs. We were looking to solve the traditional challenges brought on by disparate silos of data with separate user authentication systems and inconsistent interfaces and template designs. We spent most of 2008 building the product and then launched it for our own internal customer success communities after nine months of development.

It was a great idea, and it was in touch with the pulse of the time, so all signs pointed to its success. But it was a failure. Why?

Here are some of the mistakes we made and the lessons we learned.

➢ *We took too long to build the product.*

We spent far too long on product development. Nine months was too much time to spend on building an internal-use product, especially given the fact that we didn't have any outside beta users and thus couldn't collect any feedback from prospects. When you have an exciting idea, it's very easy to get tunnel vision, to get so wrapped up in your product that you keep thinking you need to add just one more feature to make it perfect. That can be a fatal mistake, because at the end of the day, you don't have enough feedback to achieve product/customer fit. You're essentially building a product without a market, which is a losing battle for any startup.

Based on this experience, I'm now a big proponent of launching fast and think a company should go live with its product in less than 90 days. That's not much time. And it isn't always possible to launch that fast. But having a constraint in place where the engineering effort is time-boxed really forces you to strip off functionality and deliver a minimum viable product. My advice is to get the product out the door as quickly as possible, with the bare minimum functionality required to make it useful. With that in place, work hard to acquire customers (preferably paying ones) and then learn what their needs are, and be sure to incorporate that knowledge into your opinionated product. I'd recommend taking no longer than two or three months from your initial start date to get your product into the hands of prospects, who can offer you truly objective feedback on features and functionality. Then develop your product further from there. Be prepared to iterate rapidly and often.

➢ Our product tried too hard.

We were convinced that we had created a super-product with all kinds of desirable features. It did a little bit of everything. Unfortunately, it didn't do anything exceptionally well. As an example, when we used it to replace our phpBB message board, our community went into uproar because the product lacked many of the specialized features a mature forum offers, like notifications and the ability to handle code examples in a comment.

A side effect of the feature glut was that as we made the product more and more complex, its performance degraded. In my mind, speed is an essential feature for all web apps, so this was unacceptable, especially since this app was used to run live public websites. We spent hundreds of hours trying to speed up the app with little success. This lesson taught me that we needed to have benchmarking tools incorporated into the development cycle from the beginning due to the nature of our product.

So not only had we spent too long developing a market-irrelevant product, but our product functionality was too broad! At first glance, this seems like a paradoxical problem to have—after all, the more features, the better, right? Wrong. We learned the hard way that we shouldn't try to be all things to all people but instead should focus on building an application that did a few things exceptionally well. We needed to pick our battles and try to solve one or two key problems, not twenty. The old acronym *K.I.S.S.* ("keep it simple, stupid") might sound a bit harsh, but it's nonetheless brutally accurate for startups. After learning this lesson, I have realized that the concept of swiftly delivering a minimum viable product to prospects is one of the most compelling aspects of the lean startup movement.

➤ *Our development process was not customer-centric.*

I've already mentioned how our product didn't perform up to customer expectations in several areas. Another way in which our development process wasn't customer-centric had to do with pricing. The tools we were looking to replace were pretty cheap (typically less than $100/month). We wanted to focus on small and medium-sized businesses, as that was our area of expertise, so we priced the product around $500-1,000/month. This caused another major disconnect with customers. The integration costs were typically $10,000 to migrate an existing site into our system. With such high costs of adoption, the sales cycle became prohibitively long and expensive relative to the lifetime value of the customer and the recurring revenue. Our target customer at the time (a small or medium-sized company), couldn't afford to spend that much. We quickly realized our product was not priced right, and that our model wasn't financially viable.

In hindsight, it's obvious that throughout this entire experience, our product development process was not terribly lean. We wasted a great deal of time, money, and energy by not getting something simple into the hands of prospects quickly, by failing to focus on serving a narrow niche market well before broadening our horizons, and by not adequately considering the economies of customer acquisition costs relative to the revenue generated.

> "For every failure, there's an alternative course of action. You just have to find it. When you come to a roadblock, take a detour."
> — **Mary Kay Ash**

Fortunately, we did a few things right.

ITERATION AND A STARTUP SUCCESS STORY

In the traditional startup model—the one that prevailed through the dot-com heyday—companies typically developed their product or service in secret, launched it publicly (often to great media hoopla and with a flood of cash), and sat back to wait for spectacular success. It was only in the case of spectacular failure (assuming some capital was left to spend) that changes were made to the product or business model. Often by this time it was too late, and many good business ideas died in a smoldering pile of worthless stock options.

In the lean startup model, things are done differently. Lean startup entrepreneurs tend to be a bit more realistic about what they don't know. In fact, the process is viewed as a learning experience with the customer as the teacher. And failure isn't bad—it's an opportunity to improve. To sum up this perspective: *Fail fast and often; learn quickly and inexpensively.*

My own Inc. 500 software company, Hannon Hill, currently makes mid-market web content management solutions for higher education and other industry verticals. It didn't always. The path from our original product idea to the one which finally brought us success was anything but a smooth, straight line.

When I first started the company in December of 2000, the vision was to provide a software-as-a-service (SaaS) content management application that would make it easy to update a small business website. We would charge $30 per month, and the service would work with existing websites over FTP and provide a visual interface similar to Windows Explorer, allowing users to click on a file and edit it in a browser-based word processor. Upon saving the changes, the file would then be sent over FTP back to the web server, along with a backup version. The benefits of this model included:

- No software to install on the server or web browser
- No up-front fee and a low monthly cost
- Familiar file manager interface with word processor

The software was as easy to use as web-based email. The only problem was that it was a complete failure. I learned several lessons quickly after going full-time: The market wasn't accepting of SaaS. $30 per month per site was much too cheap to build a sustainable business. Customers needed significant hand-holding to get up and running.

By August 2001, I knew that something had to change. There simply wasn't a reachable market large enough for us to be successful. We retooled the product to be an installed server application at the price point of $1,000 for a 10-user license and transitioned from software delivered as a service for a monthly fee to the traditional model of installed software purchased with a single upfront fee. To our excitement, we sold our first $1,000 license by the end of August and thought we had found a path to growth and profitability.

Over the next 24 months (the approximate life of the application), we sold a whopping 25 licenses. You don't even have to do the math to see that selling about $1,000 a month of software doesn't really make for a good business. But as a result of iterating to an installed software model, we had taken an important step toward our future success.

The 2001 Internet World Trade Show in New York City was originally scheduled to take place during the second week of September. At that time, our product was not yet mature enough to showcase at the event. But in a stroke of luck (ironically, as a result of the events of September 11th), the show was pushed back to the second week of December. We worked hard on improving our product in the interim, and as it turned out, we were able to attend. While at the trade show, we serendipitously met a much larger software company that was explicitly looking for a content management system to sell to their installed client base of over one million licensees. We had several rounds of discussions with their management team at the show and by the following spring had consummated a deal to license our product for them to sell under their own brand name. They would pay us money up front, along with a royalty for each license sold. We had our first big break!

We had a little bit of operating capital by then and enough money to finally hire our first full-time employee. But the euphoria was short-lived. By the summer of 2002, we knew that we were never going to be successful selling the product as it was at the time. We simply didn't have the resources or economies of scale to make it work.

Our next big iteration involved shifting our focus to an entirely new market segment—mid-market companies—a space in which we thought we could charge more for our product and be more competitive. We began building a completely new mid-market Java-based web content management system using the expertise we'd gained over the past few years. The unique differentiator of our new product was a combination of XML, search engine optimization, and distributed server publishing. Of course, building a next-generation product from scratch was a massive undertaking, but it allowed us to address the mistakes we made in the architecture of the first product.

We spent a year building the application in a vacuum—a luxury made possible by the pre-paid royalties we were receiving. I had not yet read Steve Blank's book, *Four Steps to the Epiphany,* which argues for customer-driven development whereby you build the product *after* you have customers telling you what they want. Not knowing any better, we didn't operate according to his model. However, we did have customers from the previous incarnation of our product, and we knew some of the things they wanted. We also knew what functionality we wanted in order to manage our own site.

We launched our new content management system on April 15, 2003 at the Internet World trade show in San Jose, CA, where we promptly won the *Best of Show* award. We received great feedback and left feeling good about things. The outlook for the new product was bright.

Unfortunately, an amazing product launch doesn't necessarily equal phenomenal sales. By the end of 2003, after working nonstop trying to sell the new application, we had only managed to sell one license. Now, selling a single server license for $30,000 (the price for our new product) sure felt better than selling a bunch of the previous lower-priced SaaS version. But selling only one license over the course of six months was still discouraging.

With the first version of the new product complete, an award under our belt, and our first full-price client (we had given away several free licenses to get early users), the next major phase in growing the company was learning how to sell and market the product. Lead generation was the first area we focused on and continuously iterated. We tried three different tactics: cold calling, channel development through partners, and Pay Per Click ads.

Cold Calling

The first cold calling strategy we had was to buy a list of all the CIOs of companies in the Southeast with revenues between $100M and $1B (a market segment often termed "mid-sized companies"). After cold-calling 1,000 organizations, we still had only managed to set up a measly four appointments. While it constituted an admirable effort, our cold calling strategy suffered from a lack of the following:

- Compelling value proposition
- Reference customers whose names we could drop
- Product or company name recognition in the market

Cold calling would eventually become one of our most effective strategies, but it took us a good 12 months to figure out precisely where we needed to focus our efforts.

Channel Development Through Partners

We had always assumed that finding implementation partners and resellers would be a logical strategy for growing the business. Potential partners, such as interactive agencies and independent software vendors, would provide the services, and we'd provide the product. Ideally, it would be a win-win situation.

It never worked.

We tried hard over the course of several years to develop partnerships with promising companies. We ended up with just 10 company relationships, which resulted in only five actual sales. Very few partners would sign on officially, and even fewer relationships ended up generating any revenue at all (and not much, at that). Additionally, it took me a long time to make the connection, but eventually I realized that our business model was undermining itself. Because agencies typically operate using a "time and materials" model, introducing a mid-market CMS to a client would then reduce the amount of money the agency could bill, since tens of thousands of dollars in CMS costs would have to come right out of the same client budget as hourly fees. From an agency's perspective, building a custom client solution (as opposed to reselling our CMS)—*even if it was more expensive and less functional*—made more sense for them, given their business model. It didn't make sense, but we had to accept that this was the reality and that we'd have to find another business strategy if we wanted to succeed. It was a hard lesson for us to learn.

Pay Per Click Ads

Pay Per Click (PPC) ads are the sponsored ads that show up alongside search results in Google and other search engines. When we did our first PPC campaign in late 2003, it was much more affordable and cost-effective compared to today. Combined with well-designed landing pages, PPC ads allowed us to generate leads from a variety of industries. We would then methodically follow up with each lead and move promising prospects through the sales funnel. By the end of 2004, we had signed at least one client representing each of the following verticals:

- Management consulting (1, from cold call)
- Healthcare (1, from cold call)
- Utilities (1, from partner)
- Hospitality (1, from partner)
- Technology (1, from PPC)
- Higher education (2, from PPC)

As we started making more sales, we noticed an emerging trend with higher education clients. It was the one vertical where we had been able to generate numerous leads using PPC ads. What's more, our application was uniquely suited to the types of challenges that higher education clients were looking to solve.

Our product's special sauce is the ability, from one single product instance, to manage multiple websites that live on multiple servers and use different operating systems. Coincidentally, colleges and universities typically have a collection of independent websites with little or no consistency, given that the development of these sites happened organically and in piecemeal fashion. Our software can handle different scripting technologies and also publish records to remote databases. Multi-site management is a hard problem to solve, so the flexibility of our product was a key differentiator for us when signing these clients. In addition, we had a simple per-CPU pricing model with unlimited sites, users, groups, and content combined with a focus on XML (before XML really hit the mainstream). All of these characteristics made our CMS seem like the perfect solution for many higher education prospects.

I wish I could say we planned it that way, but we didn't. The reason we could publish to different servers and support all the major programming languages was because of the goal we had set in our very first iteration of the CMS (the failed SaaS model): to support all small business shared hosting accounts. Because our SaaS CMS was tailored for small businesses, the only way to get content to their servers was through FTP or SFTP. There weren't any other options.

With our new mid-market CMS, we set out to provide all the benefits of a dynamic database-driven website with the performance and flexibility of being able to publish pre-assembled web pages. As it turned out, unbeknownst to us until we started signing multiple higher education clients, our product was perfect for this vertical. We now had a robust product built around a key differentiator (multi-site management), and we had amassed reference customers in a specific vertical. It was finally time to grow a serious business. At this point I had been running the business on my own for over four years and was barely scraping by. By the start of 2005, I knew we were on to something special.

Our new marketing strategy was pretty simple: We would cold call all 4,160 two-year, four-year, public, and private colleges and universities in the U.S. and Canada, targeting prospects with specific job titles that indicated responsibility for IT or communications. I had three full-time salespeople at the time, and they would make calls and set up web demos for me. My role on the call was to be both the sales engineer and the passionate product manager who gave the demo. It worked beautifully. Sales tripled in 2005 and more than doubled the following year. We had finally hit our stride.

Today we have signed more than 175 colleges and universities as clients, making us one of the top higher education CMS vendors in the world. We've also made significant inroads into other industry verticals, with dozens more clients in the government, nonprofit, healthcare, and technology sectors. At the end of the day, our success came down to the following:

- Making decisions quickly and figuring out what works and what doesn't work;

- Being passionate about the product and its market opportunities; and

- Possessing an unshakeable determination to succeed.

Had we built a simpler product in the first place, and worked more closely with our customers along the way, I think we would have arrived twice as fast. But the learning experience has been profound, and I've come to view the entire entrepreneurial process as centering on a product vision shaped by failure and iteration—a series of small advances resulting from lessons learned and customer feedback.

The lean startup model is all about iteration and evolution. While the emphasis is mine, I think Rosabeth Moss Kanter, writing for *The Harvard Business Review,* has phrased it perfectly:

> As many technology companies have seen to their peril, you can leap much too far into the future by seeking revolution, not evolution, leaving potential users in the dust. But steady progress—step by single step—can win internal support and the external race for share of market or share of mind. *Especially if you take each step quickly.*[37]

CHAPTER 9 ■ BUILDING A SALES MACHINE

I was recently talking sales strategy over lunch with an entrepreneur who has a successful consulting company. He's been in business for four years and has recruited 10 full-time consultants. He described to me a common challenge that many startup founders face: the strain of wearing multiple hats. In addition to managing his consultants and coordinating the delivery of work on existing deals, he was also constantly out in the field selling his company's services. Aside from the obvious stress that comes along with an 80-hour work week, he was constantly under tremendous pressure to go out and get new business. His quandary was that if he doesn't sign any new clients, the business will go under, and if he doesn't sell even more deals than he did last year, then the business won't grow. On top of this, he had to keep existing clients happy and make sure that his consultants were performing up to standard.

This is a tough situation to be in, but not a hopeless one. I had plenty of suggestions for him, but my strongest recommendation was to build a strong sales organization. I've learned from my own experience that a robust sales machine is at the heart of a startup's success. My other big suggestion was to hire some junior sales and marketing people to help him maximize his reach. In fact, sales assistants may well be the key to building a strong and successful sales machine, as we will see.

Assembling a good sales team is an incremental process that starts small, often with just a single sales rep or assistant hired to help you be more effective. Remember that as the founder of the company, you will always be the most knowledgeable and convincing salesperson you've got. You know the product inside and out (you probably even designed and built it), you're enthusiastic about your vision, and you have the tenacity that comes with really wanting to succeed. It makes sense, in the beginning at least, for you to be out there selling. It never really ends, not even after you've become CEO and hired a full sales team.

However, it's hard to keep pursuing new deals while you're still overseeing day-to-day operations and the myriad responsibilities that go along with wearing the management hat. Building a sales team is no easy task, and, for me at least, it can actually be more difficult than developing a solid product. Hiring successful salespeople ranks right up there as being one of the most challenging things that you'll ever do for your company, simply because it's hard to figure out ahead of time whether a particular candidate will work out in the position. Why? Salespeople are great at selling themselves, but that doesn't mean that they'll be great at selling your product or service. As you build your sales organization bit by bit, you'll quickly find that effective sales reps are worth their value many times over.

HUNTERS AND FARMERS

One of the best techniques for leveraging a startup CEO's time and energy—a tactic that has worked well for us—is adopting a tiered sales structure. This involves hiring a sales assistant to set appointments and a customer relationship coordinator (a fancy name for a sales rep) to supplement those lead generation efforts and, most importantly, to help facilitate sales. Maintaining this differentiation of responsibilities and tasks by adopting a tiered sales structure will help you maximize the returns of this cooperative relationship.

But you need to be thinking about more than just rustling up new business. Holding on to the opportunities you've already won can be just as crucial to your company's success as signing new customers. Keeping your existing clients happy and satisfied will create new possibilities for upsells, upgrades, and cross-selling opportunities, not to mention the fact that you'll have plenty of references to help you win over even more new business. Getting to this point requires consistently excellent customer service, which, from the sales perspective, involves nurturing existing clients and upselling them whenever appropriate. You'll need someone to fill this critical gap if you want a truly robust sales team.

Think about this division of labor in terms of hunters and farmers. Your sales reps, also called account executives, are like hunters. They bring in virtually all of your new business and are always on the prowl for a fresh catch. Once they go in for the kill, they have done the bulk of their work and must simply bring back their catch to receive their reward. On the other hand, your account managers (those members of your sales team who focus on ongoing customer relationships) more closely resemble farmers. They also contribute to the sales team's

success, but in a different way. The seeds they sow take the form of periodic check-ins with existing clients, suggestive upselling where appropriate, and other strategic moves designed to nurture customers and keep them happy while expanding sales opportunities. The better they do, the more bountiful the overall sales harvest will be.

When it comes to building a well-oiled sales machine, there's more to it than meets the eye. Just remember that it's not all about getting new business, and make sure you pay ample attention to existing clients and the opportunities they present. The benefits far outweigh whatever resources you invest.

KICKING IT UP A NOTCH

While it's nice to aim high with your hiring goals, expecting someone to come in and be as effective as the CEO at selling isn't really a reasonable expectation. However, setting up processes and people to make the CEO more successful at selling until the business reaches a point where the CEO is no longer needed for that role is a strategy I highly recommend. One of these crucial support roles is that of the sales assistant. Hiring a sales assistant to set and manage appointments can really facilitate growth during the seed stage of your company. The sales assistant isn't the subject matter expert that is doing the solution selling—that's probably going to be you, at least at first. Rather, this person's only responsibility is setting up appointments, in-person or via a conference call, for the lead sales rep to do the actual selling. This position doesn't require much sales experience (if any); all that's needed is pleasant phone manners and the ability to use scheduling tools. This strategy makes the most efficient and effective use of the CEO's time by minimizing the time spent chasing leads and maximizing face time with the most promising prospects.

A simple solution to getting a sales assistant in place is to hire an intern at an hourly rate to set up appointments and then pay some sort of performance compensation of $50 to $100 for every appointment completed with a prospect that fits the ideal customer profile. If this works, great! Hire someone full-time and invest in it. I've found that entrepreneurs are often paralyzed by the fear that letting anyone else sell on their behalf, especially in the early stages of the company, that they'll misrepresent the business and potentially embarrass the entrepreneur. I think this fear is unfounded. Only a small part of it is about personality; the rest is all about how well you train your sales assistants. With proper training, you'll have very little to fear. Armed with the right value proposition and a pleasantly persistent demeanor, a good sales assistant can gauge interest, set up appointments, and help start selling.

ASSEMBLING YOUR SALES MACHINE

Even with a sales assistant, as CEO you will probably still be making most or all the sales yourself until your business takes off. You may well be an army of one for quite a while when it comes to your startup's sales organization, but sooner or later the time will come when it finally makes sense to start hiring outside sales professionals. Most bootstrapping entrepreneurs wait too long to acknowledge this milestone, working a hundred hours a week and putting a strain on their health and on family relationships before they're willing to surrender any responsibility for sales. Taking off the sales hat can be a scary step, but it's an inevitable phase in the evolution of your startup and therefore is something to welcome and celebrate. The bottom line? Your business won't grow if your sales force doesn't.

The Good Salesperson Paradox

Many entrepreneurs fear hiring salespeople, and I think there's some basis for that trepidation. Because the sales personality likes to sell, he's obviously going to be pretty good at selling himself as well and will likely come across as someone who will succeed. Therein lies the central paradox you should be aware of when searching for sales reps: You want someone who's great at selling, but not so good at it that he sells you a lemon (himself). There's a fine line between the two, and it can be hard to find the right balance. What happens all too often is that we hire the best actor, not the best salesperson.

What's more, the sales personality is often unfamiliar and even alienating to other types of people. Technologists by their nature often find themselves at odds with "sales-y" types—it's the proverbial dog-cat relationship of the business world. That's not to say that your sales and engineering teams won't get along well (you should make sure they do), but it can make the hiring process more daunting for these individuals. Just as it's difficult for non-technical types to hire the right technical  people, it can also be hard to evaluate sales candidates when that's not your own area of expertise. But with the right training and techniques, anyone can learn how to effectively interview salespeople.

One piece of advice I give to entrepreneurs, especially if you're new to hiring and interviewing or if you're not a sales type yourself, is to first read Topgrading for Sales by Bradford D. Smart and Greg Alexander.[38] The book offers a systematic roadmap for a structured interview that keeps you on track and produces the information you need to make an informed decision. At my companies, we've found that Topgrading techniques can streamline the interview process and have helped us to significantly reduce costly mis-hires, thereby saving time and resources over the long run.

While interviewing salespeople is a specialized art, you can get better at it with practice. Here are some very general interviewing tips that apply specifically to hiring those first sales reps:

- **Rein in your ego.** The person you'll be hiring will *not* be replacing you or taking over the company. He or she will be assuming some responsibilities in a key area where you need help. Approach the interviewee as a mentor, not a rival.

- **Get a second opinion.** If at all possible, have a professional salesperson, a colleague or mentor who understands salespeople, or at least another cofounder sit in on the interview. This will reduce the likelihood that you'll make decisions based on subjective, but not necessarily rational, influences like physical appearance or perceived likeability. You'll be much less vulnerable to subconscious assumptions (*He talks slow; he must be lazy. She went to my alma mater; she must be smart.*).

- **Know your stuff.** Make sure you're fully acquainted with the finer points of your compensation plan structure (keep it simple!) and able to articulate it in clear detail. If your plan is attractive and fair, it will be an inducement for good candidates. If you're fuzzy on the specifics, it will send up a red flag, suggesting that you're still too green to really understand or properly execute a good plan.

- **Listen as much as you talk.** Because you're conducting the interview, you'll be asking most of the questions, but be sure to give the candidate a chance to elaborate on their answers and to ask some questions of their own. The questions that he or she has for you can go a long way towards revealing whether you're a fit for each other. Candidates who *don't* ask any questions, on the other hand, should raise suspicion. At best, they didn't care enough to prepare for the interview; at worst, they might not have the kind of inquisitive and self-starting nature that will make them a success at your company.

- **Do things differently.** Skip the by-the-book interview questions (*What is your greatest weakness?*). These kinds of questions are predictable, and most candidates will already have prepared canned answers for them. You'll learn much more about someone by asking unusual questions that require consideration on the spot and that reveal something of the candidate's nature or personality. Also require a writing sample, and kill two birds with one stone by making the prompt one that tests the candidate's knowledge about your industry and company.

- **Keep it conversational.** Pay close attention to the candidate's communication skills. The technical and analytical skills necessary for the position will vary depending on your product, but salespeople must always be articulate, persuasive, and congenial. Use this opportunity to get a sense of how they might converse with a potential client. Ideally, they'll maintain a professional yet friendly tone, and you'll be persuaded that they know what they're talking about. If they're visibly nervous during the interview, what makes you think they'll be at ease when talking to prospects?

I agree with serial entrepreneur Mark Suster when he says that the best salespeople for startups are *evangelical*. Once again, it's about selling customers a problem, not a solution. This approach is especially useful where there are already known needs and assigned budgets. Mark advises that, when looking to hire salespeople:

> The specific things you're looking for are: intelligence, ability to think creatively, ability to work with customers on vaguely defined problems, ability to assemble an ROI business case (with a template already created by marketing) and above all else the ability to listen, summarize and follow-through. Early stage selling is way more "evangelical" than process driven.[39]

Resist the VP of Sales Temptation!

When it comes to building your sales machine, if you feel lost and are seeking expert guidance, you might think that the next logical step is to hire an executive-level person to swoop in and save the day. It makes sense at first glance; after all, you've never put together a sales team before, so what do you really know about it? Maybe you're excited about your company's growth and are impatient when it comes to the slow process that hiring can often become. In situations like this, the conventional wisdom is to go find a seasoned VP of Sales to come wave a magic wand and create the perfect sales team. The reality is that this isn't always such a great idea.

The experience of a particular local startup is instructive here.

They had an innovative product and had attained a critical mass of customers, but they still hadn't fully built out their sales and marketing machine. Tempted by the lure of growth and expansion, they decided to hire an experienced executive, to the tune of $150K salary plus stock options, to take the reins. It didn't work. The newly hired VP of Sales, who had plenty of experience but had never worked with a startup before, focused almost entirely on building out channel relationships with big resellers. The problem was that those big resellers weren't actually interested in reselling because there wasn't enough market demand yet. After about a year of inertia with no real results, the startup decided to part ways with the VP of Sales. It was an expensive mistake to make, but a good learning experience nonetheless.

This is not to say that hiring a VP of Sales is never a good idea, but there's a time and a place for everything. Don't succumb to the VP of Sales temptation until you're sure you've got certain fundamentals right. I recommend having a solid inbound marketing plan in place as well as a repeatable customer acquisition process that works. You'll also need at least 10 reference customers and five case studies, and you should have two inside sales reps consistently making quota. Once you've laid this foundation, then you can think about bringing in a VP of Sales to start scaling out your sales organization. Unfortunately for the startup mentioned here, the desire to expand caused them to hire a VP of Sales prematurely, wasting time and tons of money in the process. Don't let the same thing happen to your company.

Headhunters "R" Us

If you find yourself truly overwhelmed at the prospect of finding and hiring a great sales team, there are many staffing firms that specialize in placing sales reps. The advantages to you, as far as saving time and resources in finding and vetting candidates, can be considerable—but so can the costs. Recruitment firms normally operate on contingent, retained search, or contract arrangements. With contingency and retained searches, recruiter fees are based on a percentage (usually between 20% and 35%) of the candidate's first-year compensation. If you go this route, make sure that you're clear on exactly what is meant by "compensation"—base salary only, or a percentage of the salary plus commissions and bonuses? Contract recruiters usually charge an hourly rate ranging anywhere from $50 to $150 an hour. The potential for abuse here is high, so put controls in place by setting a ceiling for charges based on the length of the search as projected by the recruiter. Whatever arrangement you decide on, if you do go with a recruiter, it's a good idea to require a guarantee, whereby candidates who don't work out will be replaced for no charge or a reduced fee.[40]

Outsourcing is another possibility for building up your sales organization, although I usually don't advise it for a young company. I hate to see startups elect to outsource their sales before learning what works and what doesn't. When you're still in the process of creating a genuine sales strategy (not to mention learning how to measure it), I think it's a mistake to turn this vital responsibility over to somebody else. Too often companies are quick to outsource what they haven't even achieved a mastery of yet.

With regard to hiring a good sales team, if you decide to go ahead and do it yourself, you'll find plenty of resources for discovering prospective candidates—the key is knowing how to attract the best ones. Remember that salespeople are motivated by financial incentives, so focus on the earning potential that awaits the right candidate. Announce the position on your company's website and through online social and professional networks like Facebook, LinkedIn, and Twitter. Use your own personal website or blog, and put feelers out among your own industry contacts and association memberships in order to get a leg up on recruiting excellent candidates. You can go through traditional job boards, including local ones as well as ones from nearby colleges and universities focused on management majors and general business majors; use the resume search features to check frequently for new resumes. But also make sure you post your ad on Craigslist, which in recent years has become one of the most popular resources for job hunters. Whatever you do, don't waste your time with juggernaut job boards like CareerBuilder and Monster, because you'll end up with mostly noise and not much signal.

MEASURING SUCCESS

One of the first things to do as part of hiring a new salesperson is to establish success milestones. These are simply goals that the sales rep should achieve during their first six to twelve months on the job, assuming you have a consultative sales process with a decent learning curve. Milestones allow you to measure the progress of the sales rep, and they enable the sales rep to pace themselves appropriately. What gets measured gets done.

Here are some categories to measure:

- Call conversations
- Demos scheduled
- Demos completed
- Opportunities created
- Opportunities closed/won

Of course, these are standard sales metrics. What I'm emphasizing here is that you need to establish specific numbers of each item that a new salesperson must meet for every 30-day period in order to stay in their position until quota is achieved. You can facilitate this by setting behavioral or activity standards, such as requiring reps to be in the office every day by 9:00 a.m., or by sending the message that missing sales meetings is unacceptable. What's most important is that you

"Sales are contingent on the attitude of the salesman — not the attitude of the prospect."

— **W. Clement Stone**

communicate your expectations clearly and enforce them fairly and consistently. Once a rep makes quota, they are no longer micromanaged, and they won't be again so long as they remain on track for quota the next time around.

GETTING THE INCENTIVES RIGHT

Calculating Sales Commissions

Sales commissions are a tricky thing. Once you put them in place, it is difficult to change them without the sales team being demoralized by the fear that their compensation is going to go down, even if this isn't the case. The goal with setting commissions, generally speaking, is to minimize base salary and to maximize performance-based compensation. Here are some thoughts on strategy:

- **Align company interests with the sales incentive structure.** Set commission percentages based on the profitability of the item being sold, such that things like license revenue have a higher percentage commission than services revenue.

- **Significantly reduce compensation if quota isn't hit.** For example, cut the standard commission in half if quota isn't reached within the designated time period.

- **Don't limit the upside.** Putting a cap on the maximum amount a sales rep or account manager can earn demotivates the salesperson and ultimately is self-defeating for the company.

Dharmesh Shah, serial software entrepreneur and author of the popular *OnStartups.com* blog, makes another important point:

> Always connect incentives somehow to ultimate customer happiness. If you reward just "deals getting done," you'll get deals—but at too high a price. You might get push-back that sales people don't control/influence customer happiness, but they do. They "pick" customers, they set expectations, they control the degree of "convincing" applied.[41]

Shah's observation is a helpful one. All too often we focus on quantity (number of deals) when we should also be encouraging quality. The main takeaway here is to make sure that your compensation structure reflects a win-win arrangement for both the company *and* the salesperson.

Sales Commissions for Subscriptions

I was talking to a very successful entrepreneur recently about how he handles sales rep compensation for a sales model involving annual service subscriptions. What I really liked about his approach was that quota was calculated on a monthly basis, whereby no commission was paid at all until 60% of quota was reached for that month. After that threshold was reached, commission was paid on all deals up to that point, and then more incentives were added on top of that as subsequently higher percentages of quota were reached. The result was that sales reps consistently worked hard and focused on signing deals instead of obsessing about their base salary.

Obviously there are different approaches that work across markets, but startups selling SaaS solutions—or any type of contract or recurring time-based service, for that matter—should also consider issues unique to their own selling proposition. One of these entails developing a way to appropriately reward sales reps for selling renewal subscriptions to existing customers. As I mentioned at the start of this chapter, while your account executives are the hunters of the sales team, your account managers correspond more closely to farmers. Their job takes patience and persistence, especially since it involves renewing existing customers as well as upselling whenever possible. They also need recognition and compensation for their different but complementary contributions to the sales machine. Consequently, you will want to be sure to set up a commission structure that will reward hunters and farmers alike.

Non-Monetary Incentives

To any discussion of sales compensation I would have to add that salespeople, like all people, also respond well to acknowledgement, recognition, and appreciation. Regardless of their job description, everyone flourishes in a workplace with a corporate culture that emphasizes and values their contributions. Yes, money is a primary motivator for salespeople, but it is also important to have non-monetary incentives in place. Here are a few of the ways we do that:

- Each month we give out a "Hero of the Month" award, in which any outstanding employee is nominated by a coworker as deserving of the title and then voted on by all team members in all departments. To serve as a symbolic reminder of this honor, we even have a quirky lawn ornament that passes from hero to hero each month.

- We also do annual awards that recognize some unique aspect of each team member. Sometimes the award names reflect genuine praise (e.g., "Most Sales in a Quarter"), but more often they're lighthearted (and usually humorous) references to people's nicknames, pastimes, and idiosyncrasies. Everybody gets one, and everybody really enjoys them. Best of all, they've been a great way to build a company culture of peer recognition and appreciation.

- We developed a mentoring program in which senior sales reps train new hires and help junior reps develop their skill set and techniques. We've found that peer-based mentoring motivates junior reps to succeed not just for monetary reasons, but because their mentor and teammates are rooting for them.

- We established a "Million Dollar Club" for sales reps

who've sold $1M in total recurring revenue. We give out fun props like giant $1 checks and wrestling championship belts to serve as a physical reminder of the achievement and the distinction that goes along with it.

- Our top sales reps get priority choice for which tradeshows they want to attend. The tradeshows in San Francisco tend to be the most desirable, but there have been several times when reps have been sent to places they actually wanted to visit.

- We like to broadcast praise and positive feedback from clients and prospects in a variety of ways, from internal office-wide emails to public announcements on Twitter. We do this when a sales goal has been met, when a particular individual has performed exceptionally well, and so on. It's quick, easy, and free, and it's just one more way of encouraging our sales reps to continue to achieve.

Don't overlook the powerful results you can bring about when you expand sales incentives beyond financial remuneration to include a range of non-monetary rewards like recognition and praise.

GETTING DOWN TO BRASS TACKS

Once you've got the beginnings of an effective sales machine in place, along with a proper incentive structure, there are a few other nuts-and-bolts processes and issues that require your attention and planning. It goes without saying that any entrepreneur would be thrilled to have tons of leads coming in, but what do you do to make sure all of them get followed up on properly? Do you have a system in place to assign those leads to sales reps in a fair and efficient manner? Do you have a uniform follow-up procedure that every sales rep will use religiously? How do you measure success once your sales team actually starts making sales, and how do you hold them accountable for future performance? When it comes to these sorts of questions—the kind that seem to come out of nowhere, when you least expect it—you'll find that thinking things through ahead of time will help you be prepared for when this moment actually arrives for your company.

Sales Territories and Assigning Leads

Sales territories allow you to define which prospects or leads are handled by specific sales reps. While they're a common and admittedly straightforward way to decide which salesperson gets which leads, territories aren't the only way to assign leads. Here are some ways you can divvy up leads among members of your sales team:

- By geographical territories (e.g., region, country, state, city, zip code, telephone area code, or some combination of these)

- By industry verticals or company type such that certain industries (e.g., technology, government, energy, etc.) are owned by specific reps

- By company size, which can be based either on the number of employees or total revenues of the prospect company

- Through round robin so that each lead that comes in (or list that is generated) is handed to the next sales rep in sequential order

We have found that the "round robin" model works best for us, mainly because it is the most random and fair. Other companies may find that assigning leads based on set territories makes more sense for their product or sales model. Territories can be a complex challenge for a fast-growing company, though, because you're likely to encounter morale issues if you're constantly changing how leads are assigned to your sales team, especially if some reps feel that the system is unfair or takes leads away from them. It's just human nature to fear change and expect the worst. Choosing a lead distribution strategy and creating territories are both critical decisions for startups and should not be taken lightly.

Setting a Sales Quota

Setting sales quotas can be a challenging exercise, but it will undoubtedly be a great learning experience for first-time CEOs. After doing some research and getting advice from mentors and entrepreneur friends, my own experience with determining quota structure still needed some tweaking before I got it right. Lots of trial and error has shown me that the ideal arrangement has the majority of the compensation coming from commissions, with a common split being 40% salary and 60% commission for the targeted earnings figure. You'll have to experiment to see what works best for you.

For us, one of the most effective strategies we employ to determine sales quotas begins with choosing the appropriate On Target Earnings (OTE) for the type of sales rep that makes sense for both the product and the market. OTE equals the base salary plus commission for hitting quota in a calendar year. Here are some examples that will illustrate how this works:

- Sales rep who handles mostly inbound leads for a product that isn't too complex: $30K base + $20K commissions = $50K OTE

- Sales rep who cold calls and works inbound leads with a semi-complex product: $30K base + $50K commissions = $80K OTE

- Sales rep who sells a complex product face-to-face, requiring extensive travel: $100K base + $100K commissions = $200K OTE

Once you've determined the type of rep you need, the nature of a typical sale, and your desired OTE, figuring out the quota based on commissions should be a simple math exercise. You will probably find that it takes a few tries before you perfect your quota and commission structure, but the best advice I can give is to get OTE right and make commissions fair with no cap on total earnings.

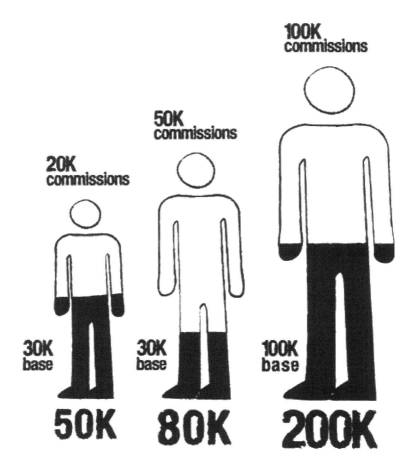

Supporting Your Sales Team

Building a professional sales organization and equipping your sales team with the tools and support they need to be effective pose some of the most fundamental challenges an entrepreneur must face. Here are some of the most important lessons I've learned over the years in regard to how you can support your sales team:

- **Give your reps sales-ready leads.** It may take some time for your startup to arrive at an accurate definition of a sales-ready lead, but sales and marketing teams must work together to make sure everyone is on the same page. One of the chief complaints salespeople voice about the sales funnel is that marketers put quantity ahead of quality when it comes to leads. Having to sort through scads of poor-quality leads wastes time and phone calls, thereby reducing the sales rep's effectiveness. Your sales team will do their best work if they're only given qualified leads that are sales-ready. If a lead is passed to the sales team prematurely, it should be immediately returned to the marketing team to be put on an automated nurturing program until that lead *is* sales-ready.

- **Adopt a CRM process.** There are many affordable customer relationship management (CRM) solutions out there from companies like salesforce.com and SugarCRM with all the bells and whistles you need. The important thing is documenting what is expected of sales reps as well as the sales manager, and then defining CRM usage standards. It is very difficult for a company to plan or manage growth if the CRM is not truly adopted by the sales organization. One way to do this is to require that data be entered in the CRM as a prerequisite for commission payout.

- **Provide clearly defined BANT criteria.** Maintaining a clear and consistent definition of BANT (Budget, Authority, Need, and Timeline) is critical for creating opportunities in the sales pipeline. Your language must be consistent so that sales reps and management understand how deals are measured. Too often, misunderstandings about or different interpretations of these characteristics cause serious problems within an organization.

- **Implement a two-tiered sales process.** My friend Phil Hill, cofounder of VoIP company Vocalocity, has always advocated the two-tiered sales approach. After having numerous discussions with me on this topic, he convinced me that my own company needed to give the two-tiered sales process a try. I've been impressed with the results. In the two-tiered approach, Tier 1 reps are responsible

for cold calling and setting appointments for the Tier 2 reps, who give the initial demo and then help the prospect through the sales process until they close the deal. There's so much latent demand that is left dormant when cold-to-close reps chase the most promising opportunities, letting plenty of other promising leads slip through the cracks. Inevitably, when things get busy, prospecting to load the top of the funnel gets neglected in favor of closing sales with late-stage prospects. I'm a big believer in playing to someone's strengths rather than trying to shore up their weaknesses. Because the two-tiered sales process allows for specialization, I've found that it really lets the most talented and experienced sales reps focus on what they do best: closing deals.

- **Establish a performance appraisal system.** It might seem like I'm stating the obvious, but performance improves when performance is measured. Performance measurement and appraisal not only helps the sales team by continually clarifying performance targets, but it also holds people accountable for generating results. Appraisal systems are most effective when their intent is not merely to police performance, but to help your sales team improve in those areas that make the biggest possible impact on the business. A good performance appraisal program is an excellent tool for helping entrepreneurs and managers monitor and support the performance of their sales teams.

- **Continuously iterate while developing the sales team.** Remember that agile methodologies can apply to building a sales organization, too. Iterate! Implement new processes once they've been shown to work. Continually refine and improve your demo scripts, your presentation slides, and any other sales collateral that your team employs. Share strategies and techniques of your best-performing salespeople and spread them throughout the sales organization.

- **Support your team with training and coaching.** Motivational speaker Zig Ziglar has said that salespeople need to commit to a lifetime of training, and I completely agree. I've found that successful salespeople are almost always eager to participate in training and coaching. Sales education today comes in many forms and through a variety of channels, from professional offsite seminars and online webinars, to books, audio courses, and podcasts. All of these forms of training are valuable and should be encouraged, but nothing takes the place of providing specific, detailed training on your own products—and your competitors' offerings as well—and an overview of the particular sales challenges within your own market. We recently added weekly sales workshops to our own training program. They work much like our manager trainings, wherein we each come up with a few topics we'd like to discuss, write them all down, and then pick two each week to conduct experience sharing sessions around (e.g. prospecting, gatekeepers, etc).

The Value of a Well-Oiled Sales Machine

It goes without saying that having a good product is fundamental to your company's success. But it's not that simple—you also have to sell that product. No matter how great it is, and no matter how awesome your customer service is, your product isn't going to sell itself. You need an efficient and effective sales machine in place to take care of that.

Building that sales machine is no easy task. In fact, it may be one of the most difficult things you undertake as an entrepreneur. There are many things to consider: when to hire, who to hire, how to motivate them, and how to compensate them. Just think of these factors as the maintenance and upkeep that you must do in order to ensure your sales machine stays well-oiled and runs efficiently.

The two-tiered model that I champion here has worked well for me, but it's just one possible approach you can take. You'll have to undergo some trial and error before you find the right configuration for your own company's sales machine. Hopefully this chapter will set you on the right path to learning what works best for you.

CHAPTER 10 ▪ IF YOU BUILD IT, WILL THEY COME?

You might have heard the common entrepreneurial axiom, generally attributed to American thinker and essayist Ralph Waldo Emerson: "Build a better mousetrap, and the world will beat a path to your door." While this is undoubtedly a great inspirational metaphor about innovation, it doesn't really tell the whole story. Emerson was brilliant, all right, but he was no businessman. Most entrepreneurs learn quickly (and sometimes the hard way) that he got this one wrong. The truth is, it's not enough to build an awesome mousetrap. Because a mousetrap—any mousetrap, even the best mousetrap imaginable—in and of itself will *not* actually bring the world to your door, nor will it automatically generate business or guarantee your company's success. To borrow a quote from the classic film, *Field of Dreams*: You can go ahead and build it, but you can't guarantee that they'll come.

The "better mousetrap" adage might make a good motivational slogan, but its greatest weakness is the conspicuous absence of any mention of a marketing plan. Without a clearly defined market, a good strategy, and a compelling message, your killer mousetrap won't go far.

SAY WHAT YOU MEAN, AND MEAN WHAT YOU SAY

I'm not one of those clever advertising virtuosos who can churn out catchy slogans and slick ad copy at the drop of a hat. In my own experience, learning how to get messaging right has been an iterative process, just like everything else. Much of it involves trying on different approaches for size until you find one that works. Nevertheless, for what it's worth, I'll share my own lessons learned on how to get your marketing message right:

- **Don't try to appeal to everybody.** The first and perhaps the most fundamental rule of messaging is to know your audience. It might seem smart to try and appeal to as broad a market as possible, but this approach will hurt you in the long run. Trying to address everyone all at once with a single message only creates white noise and could potentially alienate your target audience. Be selective in who you approach. The sooner you can segment your market and begin to profile your ideal customer, the sooner your marketing message will stop falling on deaf ears and start reaching people that want to hear it. Personally, I believe that every business, even the corner grocery, has a target market. If you sincerely believe that your product really *does* have universal appeal and application, I have no advice for you, except to warn you that you'll likely need a massive marketing budget, not to mention a superhuman degree of persistence, in order to accomplish your aims. More about targeting your message later.

- **Focus on value, not features.** The technical cofounder and anybody working on your development team will naturally describe your product in terms of the great features that it delivers, but don't fall into this trap. Your marketing message needs to reflect the *value* that those features bring to your customers. Too many technology startups are myopic, wasting messaging power on feature descriptions and the esoteric details of how the thing is built. Your customers couldn't care less—they just want to know what's in it for them, and

rightfully so. Focus instead on describing the benefits of using the product, why customers would find those features valuable, and so on. Demonstrate value and you're halfway there.

- **Keep it clear, clean, and jargon-free.** Your marketing message, especially your highest-level messaging, must be easy to understand from the get-go. Leave out the meaningless buzzwords and sales-speak, and don't even think about confusing your audience with a bunch of technical terms. You want to be simple but not simplistic, clean without being sparse, and direct without being pushy. Test your message internally. Until every employee, your spouse, and even your kids can easily understand just what it is you're trying to convey, then it probably needs a little more fine-tuning.

- **Talk about what you can do, not who you are.** By the same token, your main messaging goal should not involve announcing your arrival or educating the world on your company's history. Potential customers don't come to your site to read the exciting backstory of how your company was started out of your garage. They're trying to solve a problem and hoping you can help them. This can also be said of your honors and accreditations. While you may indeed have bragging rights, restrict them to your "About Us" page. They don't belong at the center of your marketing message. Your customers don't buy from you because you're a PMP, an MBA, or a PhD. They buy because you speak to their pain or their problem.

- **Follow through on message effectiveness.** You'll

obviously be logging customer inquiries and contacts from the very beginning, not to mention any sales you make. You know that for these folks, your messaging worked. But to find out what it will take to convince on-the-fence prospects who have not bought anything yet, it's very helpful to know how your message is being received by those prospects who end up choosing a competitor over you—what about your messaging *didn't* win them over? The fastest and most economical way for a cash-strapped startup to figure out if messaging is working is to start soliciting feedback very early on. The internet has made it pretty easy to test, refine, and iterate your message through the use of forums, polls, questionnaires, surveys, and other tools. SurveyMonkey and Zoomerang are some of the best ones to use for conducting your own market research and customer opinion polls on the cheap.

- **Turn employees and customers into evangelists.** As CEO, you will undoubtedly be the single best prepared, most persuasive, and ultimately most effective spokesperson for your company and its offerings. But don't stop your marketing efforts there. Even before you're big enough to hire a marketing director or department, you can still recruit your existing employees and team members to tap their own networks and influence in order to help extend your message's reach and impact. Encourage everyone on the team to make comments on social networking sites like Facebook and Twitter, to participate in relevant blogs and forums, and to write guest posts in blogs or newsletters. Be sure everyone is on the same page regarding your marketing message, but let individuals be as creative as they like in spreading the word. If your employees are as enthusiastic about your product as you are, it will speak volumes about your company. In sufficient quantities, employee evangelism could very well end up being even more convincing than you on your own. If you can get your clients to be evangelists too, then all the better! Nothing speaks louder to the strengths of a company than a happy customer who can't stop talking about you.

Crafting a great marketing message isn't easy, and it won't happen overnight. And that's only half the battle—getting the word out poses a real challenge of its own. Even though they're just a start, the principles we've covered here should help you get a leg up on the process. Remember: At the end of the day, it's not about the mousetrap. It's about solving the pains, problems, and needs of your target market.

THE BEST WAY TO CATCH AN ELEPHANT

Not long ago, marketers talked about dividing their marketing efforts into "push" and "pull" strategies. *Push marketing*, as the term suggests, involves pushing the intended message toward as large an audience as possible, in the hopes that you'll catch the attention of a few solid prospects. Push marketing vehicles include trade shows, seminars, email blasts, cold calling, outsourced telemarketing, and traditional offline sources like print advertising, billboards, and commercial media broadcasting. *Pull marketing*, on the other hand, aims to attract customers who are already in the market for a product or service similar to yours. Its goal is to be in the right place at the right time, ready and waiting with the perfect solution when the customer shows up, either in search of information or ready to buy. Pull marketing has exploded with the rise of the web; examples include search engine optimization (SEO), pay per click (PPC) campaigns, directory listings, and ecommerce portals. As of late, the more recent terms, *inbound* and *outbound*, have overtaken the traditional terminology, but the concepts are essentially the same.

Depending on the nature of your business, you might require a mix of marketing strategies, but for startups hoping to maximize their limited marketing budget while minimizing the learning curve for finding what actually works, inbound techniques are not only more cost-effective but are also becoming increasingly efficient, giving you better bang for your buck.

Plenty of observers have likened the lead generation process to trying to catch an elephant. The conventional way of doing this (outbound marketing) is to chase after elephants in the

hopes of catching a few of them. But as marketing teams have evolved, they've adopted more sophisticated inbound marketing techniques that depend on having a great website with fresh content. Think of your website as a lush watering hole in the middle of the savannah. What thirsty elephant could possibly resist? It's much easier to attract a herd of willing elephants to your watering hole than it is to chase down even one or two of them. Besides, it takes less effort and is also more cost-effective to focus on building a spectacular watering hole than it is to continue launching multiple elephant hunting expeditions with mixed results. Sales reps who hunt the old way might snag one or two elephants, but they'll exhaust themselves doing it. Make the elephants come to you instead.

Don't Neglect Your Social Life

While hyping the value of social media networks to B2C companies these days goes without saying, B2B companies have been much more reluctant to see social media as providing a "watering hole" of opportunity. The B2B model simply doesn't lend itself as well to viral campaigns that result in stampeding hordes of excited customers. Adam Blitzer, my co-founder at Pardot, concedes this in an informative blog post examining this very topic, but he argues that B2B companies shouldn't underestimate the opportunities that social media outlets provide for facilitating dialogue among customers. Although your message will be targeting a smaller audience whose fundamental similarity is their industry or business, Blitzer explains, social media messaging operates on the same axioms because it is "a web-based dialog [wherein] customers are simultaneously interacting with your brand while providing a large-scale, low-cost online focus group."[42] Many of the bigger technology companies create this type of focus group by implementing social media into their own corporate websites through an internal platform. Others populate their websites with content that is specifically geared toward social media and online networking, through channels such as ITtoolbox Community Hub, where IT professionals can discuss different vendors via blog posts, topic-based groups, and online forums.

Whether you decide to take the internal or external approach, or some combination of both, the key to getting the most out of social media lies in leveraging the ability of this new technology to generate user feedback. Facebook immediately comes to mind and is probably the easiest channel with the widest audience, but it's certainly not the only game in town. There are other channels that are well-suited to particular industries or products, but just for starters, I'd advise any startup or young company to create and actively update accounts on the following networks:

- Twitter
- LinkedIn
- Google+

- YouTube (for video content)
- Flickr (for graphic content)
- Slideshare (for presentations)

Creating accounts on all of these networks is easy, and it's free. There's really no excuse not to do it. Just make sure you consistently add your company website to all of your profiles on social media sites. Some social networking sites also allow you to link to RSS (Really Simple Syndication) feeds of your blog. Adding these links will generate more visits both to your blog and to your website. It's a no-cost and minimum-effort way that you can quickly maximize your startup's exposure.

There's no question that more and more B2B companies are coming around to the value of social media as a marketing tool. Here are just a few recent statistics that indicate which way the wind is blowing:

- Forrester predicts B2B interactive marketing spending on social media outlets like Facebook and Twitter will reach $4.8B by 2014, nearly doubling the 2009 estimate ($2.3B).[43]

- Facebook now has over 850 million active users who spend 700 billion minutes per month logged in.

- Two-thirds of comScore's U.S. Top 100 websites and half of comScore's Global Top 100 websites have integrated with Facebook.

- Facebook has already outstripped email in terms of worldwide reach, and the *company/brand/product* category is now the largest single category of Facebook pages.[44]

Despite all of these rosy statistics on the virtues of social media, there's still a surprising amount of resistance on the part of B2B entrepreneurs to embracing it as a marketing tool. To reap the full benefits of social media marketing, you must become an active participant in the conversation. Admittedly, it can take some serious time and effort before you're able to acquire a decent number of followers to converse with on platforms like Twitter, but I've found that social media offers a great deal of value with regard to generating leads and building brand awareness, spotting emerging trends, learning about competitors and complementary products, and—perhaps most importantly—developing stronger relationships with customers, partners, and friends. But none of this will happen unless you put in the effort. It might sound simplistic, but it's worth pointing out that if you're not in the conversation, your voice cannot and will not be heard. The marketing and research opportunities that social media affords have never before been available on such a massive scale at such a miniscule cost. I can personally confirm that social media marketing represents some of the best value for the money for any cash-strapped startup. B2B firms, as Blitzer warns in his blog, "should latch onto this trend while it still represents a competitive advantage, rather than a necessity for their company's survival."[45]

BAKING BREAD IN THE BLOGOSPHERE

Blogging can seem like slogging compared to other strategies that yield immediate measurable results, such as PPC campaigns and email blasts. But search engines really like blogs because of their relevant and frequently updated content. What's more, the advent of RSS feeds has made it easier than ever to increase the reach and visibility of any blog. (If you doubt the possibilities inherent in blogging, you should talk to Arianna Huffington, whose widely-read *Huffington Post* started out rather modestly as a blog.)

Linking to other pages on your site and to external sites is another way you can improve your blog's visibility. The steeper the learning curve for your product or service, the more valuable your blog can become, since it provides an ideal platform you can use to educate your readers about your company and its products as well as industry news or best practices. Even if it involves spotlighting or linking to competitors and other relevant companies, adding outbound links will enhance your site's content. The real gold, however, comes in the form of inbound links to your site from other reputable sites. These links are very valuable in that they will significantly boost your page rank and search engine results. SEOmoz offers an arsenal of great tools that delve into page rankings and similar metrics to help you keep the link juice flowing. I'll have more about search engine optimization (SEO) in a moment.

Blogging is a great method for establishing yourself as an articulate professional, a problem solver, and, ultimately, an expert in your industry. If you create good content consistently and use topically focused pages with the right keywords and phrases, you'll elevate your search engine ranking and increase the likelihood that visitors will find your product or service. Using good links in your blog will also work wonders for your rankings. As an inbound technique, though, it's important to remember that blogging is a social and search engine-focused means of getting found and known. Content should appeal to your target market, but a blog post shouldn't read like a commercial or an advertisement. It should be a conversation between you and your prospects and customers. Pose questions, air opinions, and share anecdotes—just remember to use good keywords and linking wherever appropriate, and make sure you're writing about relevant topics on a regular basis.

There's no denying that blogging involves a significant time and energy commitment if you want to see real results. You may want to consider forming a team to share responsibility for creating content. With lots of free software out there (WordPress is the best at the moment), there is not much downside to getting started and learning as you go until you're ready for a custom blog site.

All of this aside, it bears repeating that content really is king, so whatever else you do with your blog, make sure that you're posting as often as possible. I post to my personal blog (davidcummings.org) every day, although several times a week is usually a good goal to start with. Jumping right into it will help you establish your company's online presence, and the longer you do it, the more authority you will amass in your industry. But aside from the obvious PR and marketing benefits of maintaining a blog, I've surprisingly found lots of personal benefits to blogging. Here are a few reasons why I write each day:

- Writing something short every day is actually easier than writing one lengthy piece each week.

- Each day, the blogging process requires about 15-30 minutes of solid reflection on something interesting that I experienced, observed, or read in the previous 24 hours. Writing on the topic of the day helps clarify my thinking about that subject going forward.

- I've made plenty of mistakes over the years and while I view these as great learning experiences, I'd like for other entrepreneurs to not have to repeat them. To this point, my blog is a great outlet for sharing little anecdotes and tidbits of advice.

- Documenting my thoughts helps employees and business partners understand my approach and thinking.

- If I get hit by a bus, I want my kids to know my thoughts on business and life.

I highly recommend writing a daily blog post for these reasons, as well as for the obvious benefits to your company's visibility and credibility. The biggest challenge is getting through the first 30 days. After about a month, writing a daily post becomes an almost automatic routine, like brushing your teeth before bed. Once you get used to it, you won't want to stop.

Think of blogging as your site's very own content bakery. Your customers want delicious piping-hot content, baked fresh daily. Bake only once in a while and see how far you get by keeping your shelves stocked with stale bread on a regular basis; people will stop coming to your bakery! Similarly,

just as irrelevant content can kill a blog, your bakery won't do well if you start offering products like socks or jewelry. People expect to come to your bakery for quality baked goods, not for random items they'd typically buy elsewhere. Finally, your fresh content needs to be interesting, and you need to change it up enough to keep people coming back to see what's new on the menu. It's not enough to sell white bread and only white bread every day; you should have several different varieties of breads, perhaps with a daily special, and then maybe some muffins and cookies as well. A range of appropriate offerings will attract a wide audience of loyal repeat customers. All of these same principles hold true for your blog. Treat it like you would a bakery: publishing fresh content daily, staying specialized enough to be relevant to your traffic, and always having a few new and interesting things on offer.

SEO: MORE THAN JUST KEYWORDS

The best practices for how to rank well with search engines are straightforward, but it is amazing how many sites don't really address the basics. Having a company blog is essential, but beyond that, it also helps to have a separate industry-specific blog that is company-agnostic but still has links back to your company site. This blog could deal with general industry news and best practices or some sort of relevant topic, but should not report on company-specific items. The domain name should incorporate the most important search term so that it will show up high in the results for generic searches for that term or topic.

> *Variety of Content*

I already talked about the importance of having fresh, relevant, frequently updated content on your blog, but don't forget that blogs aren't the only kind of content for your site. White papers, webinars, and video content are all great forms of content, and the range of media will keep your site interesting. Write for humans, not computers—this goes for any content. The "bots" that crawl websites to index content for search engines have gotten sophisticated enough that you can no longer trick them with a page full of keywords or recycled content. Adding relevant videos to your site is another quick and easy way to boost your SEO. Video content shows up in video searches, which will only add to your rankings.

➤ *Standards-Compliant Pages*

On a similar note, ensure that your site's pages are well-formed and standards-compliant so as to demonstrate to search engines that you care about the quality of your HTML. Include a sitemap that links to all the relevant pages. Use a content management system that is conducive to good search engine results (one that employs good HTML and human-friendly URLs with keywords).

➤ *Good Titles and Headings*

Coming up with good titles and headings is a crucial part of SEO. Make sure that the most important search term is included in the first word(s) in the title of the homepage. Keep the title and largest heading (h1) present and consistent on the all pages. Your site's title and tagline are the first things visitors will notice in search results, so it's good to have a common search term that you have made unique in some way. For example, to revisit the bakery metaphor, would you rather click on a search result that simply says "Bakery homepage" or one that reads "Bob's

Bakery: Fresh-baked bread every day"?

> ## *Link Juice*

Earlier I mentioned the SEO benefits of including quality links in your blog as well as getting inbound links to your site from other reputable sites. Participate in forums and other social media (Twitter, Facebook, LinkedIn, et. al.) on a daily basis, and be sure to link back to your site wherever relevant and permitted. Comment on prominent blogs and link to your website in your signature. Ask your company's partners and resellers to link back to your site using appropriate keywords.

There are plenty of SEO tips and tricks that will help you get your site to show up higher in search engine results. But SEO is a dynamic art, so you must always keep up with how search engine algorithms change so you can alter your strategy accordingly. At the end of the day, though, content is *still* king. The bottom line is that the best way to get found by search engines is to publish fresh, quality content on a weekly, if not daily, basis.

SITE MARKETING: IT'S NOT ROCKET SCIENCE

Your number one tool for selling your product or service, not surprisingly, is your company's website. Most startup entrepreneurs realize this intuitively and yet still end up designing (or paying someone else to design) confusing sites that have such a bad user interface that it's difficult even tell what they're trying to sell! There is a world of advice out there on designing a great website, and there are plenty of technical experts you can hire to do just that. But the truth is, it's not rocket science. The design fundamentals of a successful site are relatively few in number, and anybody can use them as guidelines to create a reasonably well-designed website. A good website should be:

- **Clear, clean, and uncluttered**. Flash intros, cool music, animated gifs, and other digital gimmicks don't have a place on your website. They will distract your visitors, making it harder to find your content or even to understand what your site is selling. A clean and uncluttered site with an obvious call to action will give you the best results when it comes to converting visitors into promising leads.

- **Easy to read**. Every element of a good site—color contrast, typefaces, font size and style, and graphic images—should work for, not against, readability. Stock photos add little value to your visual message if they're not directly relevant to your business. As most of us know, bolded all-caps text is the online equivalent of uncouth yelling, and using weird fonts in a rainbow of colors will annoy your site's visitors. Keep things simple and easy to read.

- **Easy to navigate**. Today's websites typically adhere to one of several popular layouts, and there's no reason not to capitalize on that familiarity. You don't want your site to look so different from page to page that visitors think they've been sent to a completely different site each time click a link. Navigation should be intuitive and coherent from page to page, and there should be consistency between graphical and design elements on different parts of your site.

- **Valuable to the visitor**. A site that's valuable to its visitor offers content that is current, applicable, and informative. Content is always king. Your website should also value potential customers by not wasting their time with typos, broken links, poorly designed forms, and frustrating error messages. Think of the kind of site *you* would want to visit, and then build that site.

Granted, I have simplified what can be a very complicated and nuanced process. Working on the company website is one of the most highly iterative processes in any business these days, so try different things to find out what works best. But the fundamentals I've listed above hold true for any website.

EMAIL MARKETING: AN EFFECTIVE INBOX

Nowadays companies that don't use email as part of their marketing and customer relationship strategy are few and far between. According to the 2011 Chief Marketer Lead Generation

Study, 85% of respondents will be using email as a key component of their lead generation efforts in 2011, which is up from just over 80% in their 2010 survey. It would appear that email has become part of the marketing standard across the board.[46]

But despite the growing popularity of email marketing, many companies still don't follow the most basic design best practices when it comes to building email templates. Here are some of the most critical email design best practices:

- **Emails should be clean and streamlined.** If you've got a solid and relevant message, you don't need to hide it behind fancy fonts or complicated formatting. Keep it simple for maximum impact.

- **Emails should clearly communicate main points, even when skimmed quickly.** If a recipient skims the email for just 10 seconds, you still want them to absorb the same main points that a more careful reader would, so make sure your key messaging is obvious and straightforward in its presentation. Use visual cues like bullet points and bolded keywords and headings to help time-pressed readers easily sort out your email's most important takeaways.

- **Emails should focus on textual content and use images sparingly (if at all).** The majority of email clients have images turned off by default, so design for that lowest common denominator. Besides, if your message is convincing, you really don't need a graphic to drive your point home. Also, consider sending text-only emails, especially for B2B audiences.

- **Emails should look great in preview mode.** Preview panes are typically only a few hundred pixels tall. Keep this in mind when designing your emails so you can be sure that the message's lead-in looks as good as it reads.

Developing an effective email creative is critical, but all email campaigns should be subject to what I like to call the "four Ts"— tailoring, testing, timing, and tracking. *Tailor* emails to your audience by making sure they contain helpful information that's specifically geared to those recipients. *Test* those emails to make sure they render properly in all email clients. *Time* your email blasts for when they're most likely to get read—many studies suggest that lunchtime on a weekday is a great time for B2B emails, since most people check their email when returning from lunch. *Track* the emails you send out to collect metrics such as opens and click-through rates, as this data will help you design more effective emails going forward.[47]

MARKETING AUTOMATION: THE NEXT FRONTIER

Once you've jumped on the website and email marketing bandwagon, you'll find that you're dealing with a lot of different tools, each with multiple functions and aims. It can be intimidating for anybody, much less a first-time entrepreneur leaping headfirst into the task of marketing a startup company and its product. But how do you go about keeping everything straight? The relatively new field of marketing automation holds the answer.

The idea behind marketing automation is to consolidate many of the traditionally disparate marketing tools into a single web-based product—sort of a one-stop-shopping experience for marketers. A good marketing automation solution will help you coordinate these tools and use them in tandem for maximum effectiveness. Depending on the solution you choose, a typical marketing automation platform will integrate most or all of the following tools and functions:

- **Email marketing,** including support for email blasts and other broadcast emails such as newsletters and one-off campaigns.

- **Landing pages,** which are webpages that are optimized for converting visitors into prospects, usually via a form.

- **Forms,** which are comprised of fields that capture prospect data when visitors enter their information, often in exchange for items like white papers, free trials, webinar sign-ups, and so on.

- **CRM integration,** which involves bi-directional connection to and syncing with common customer relationship management systems such as salesforce.com, SugarCRM, NetSuite, and Microsoft Dynamics CRM.

- **Lead scoring and grading,** including automatic scoring of prospects based on their activities as well as grading based on explicit data points about the prospect relative to the ideal customer profile.

- **Drip programs,** which consist of periodic emails and activities triggered by specific actions and timed events. For example, if a prospect clicks a certain link, they are removed from the list and the appropriate sales rep notified, and Email A is sent. If they don't click that link, then they'll get follow-up Email B in 10 days.

- **Automation rules,** which are powerful logic-driven conditionals that can change scores, trigger email sends, move prospects between lists, notify sales reps, and so on, based on a variety of criteria.

- **Anonymous visitor ID,** which provides data about individual visitors to your site, such as the visitor's company based on their IP address, so that a sales rep knows that someone at that company is potentially interested and can then follow up accordingly.

- **Prospect tracking,** including individual lead tracking of all prospect activities, such as visits to your site, webpages viewed and length of time for each, forms completed, whitepapers downloaded, email opens and click-throughs, and so on.

- **Closed loop ROI reporting,** which helps you track money spent on every stage of the sales process, from lead generation through closed deals, so that you can measure the success of marketing campaigns, even where there's a long sales cycle.

Other common functionalities include file hosting, lists,

segmentation wizards, and paid search integration. The ultimate goal is to adopt one single platform that replaces legacy systems like email marketing tools and form managers while adding significant new functionality like one-to-one tracking and reporting.

Marketing automation platforms are typically offered as a hosted SaaS solution ranging in price from $500 to $5000 per month, and some providers don't require a contract with subscription. For startups looking for value in a tight economy, these costs may seem prohibitive, but the costs of *not* adopting a marketing automation solution may be far greater. In the end, sales and marketing teams (especially small teams working on limited budgets) will on the whole be much more effective with marketing automation, which puts you in the marketing driver's seat and integrates all of your efforts from inbound channels.

In the interest of full disclosure—and just in case you missed this information in a previous chapter—I should point out that one of the companies I co-founded, Pardot, is a marketing automation software vendor. But even if that wasn't the case, I would still advise startups just go ahead and spend the money on a good solution. You will see real results.

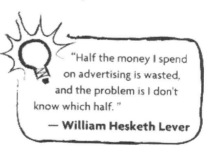

"Half the money I spend on advertising is wasted, and the problem is I don't know which half."

— **William Hesketh Lever**

PULLING IT ALL TOGETHER

We've covered a good bit of ground in this chapter. Once you've designed an awesome website with great content and a constantly updated blog, firmly established your social media presence, and fine-tuned your SEO and PPC efforts, your startup will surely be getting plenty of attention. But for inbound marketing strategies to really succeed, your efforts shouldn't end there. Your company's website must engage visitors sufficiently before it can convert them to identifiable sales leads through the information they provide by way of online forms. Once you've generated some leads, a drip email marketing campaign will "nurture" those prospects until they're ready to buy. Ideally, you don't want you or your startup's sales team to be wasting time on non-sales-ready leads. But on the other hand, you don't want to waste your marketing resources, either. A solid lead nurturing strategy strikes a happy medium and lets you stretch your resources to the best extent possible. There may well be other outbound techniques in your marketing arsenal, and locating and refining your target market will be an ongoing iterative process. I'm convinced that a combination of inbound and outbound techniques provides the best way, particularly for web-enabled startups, to get the message out about your mousetrap. Only then will the world start beating a path to your door.

CHAPTER 11 ▪ CORPORATE CULTURE IS KEY

One of the hottest topics in the business media today is corporate culture—what it is, how important it is, and how to build a strong one. Theories of organizational culture have been around since the 1970s, but the notion of a company having its own distinct culture, one that should be consciously built and nurtured to ensure the company's success, is a relatively new idea that has emerged and developed over the past two decades. Corporate culture is composed of a collection of workplace values, symbols, behaviors, and practices. It can be as simple as references to "the way we do things around here" or complex enough to involve things like office-wide rituals, a culture book with anecdotes, celebrations of company values, and so on.

I doubt that many entrepreneurs do a whole lot of thinking about corporate culture when they're just starting out. In the early stages of a startup, the whole notion of corporate culture is a futuristic pie-in-the-sky abstraction—something to be figured out well down the road, at about the same time that you'll start working on the corporate retirement plans. It's almost surreal to think that you'll have such a thing as company culture when your startup hasn't even become a company in its own right yet.

Most first-time entrepreneurs tend to assume that success must necessarily precede the genesis of a distinct corporate culture. Ironically, it's the other way around. Corporate culture takes shape in the embryonic stages of a company, and in these cases, that company culture strongly influences the growth and future success of the company itself. A strong corporate culture has been the driving force behind startups that have grown into very powerful, high-profile companies as a result. If you think for a minute about the typical characteristics of the startup environment, you'll see what I mean.

Startups typically have high-energy environments, and they're usually, almost by necessity, highly creative places to work. People have what they really need to succeed (state-of-the-art laptops) and don't seem to be deterred by what they lack (the legendary

Amazon.com door-desks provide an illustrative example here). And because startups are not yet burdened with bureaucracies and politics, there is little or no emphasis on official job titles or protocol. The rules are often made up on the fly, and processes are based on what works, since there's often no manual to go by. Obeying conventions and formalities doesn't really jibe with the startup ethos of figuring things out as you go. What *does* seem to be universally present in startups, however, is an atmosphere infused with genuine passion and drive. Folks may be working long, odd hours in shorts and flip-flops, but everybody is working *hard* at what they do best and in a spirit of collaboration rather than competition. It's not yet a case of *Me vs. You*—it's more like *All of us against the World*.

The Benefits of Being Weird

I'll admit that I'm idealizing things a bit. The important fact I've neglected to point out is that most startups are small. They don't involve that many people or that many processes, so it comes as no surprise that a complex bureaucracy is neither possible nor necessary. When there are just two of you coding all night long in your dorm room, of course you'll be pulling all-nighters! When your team of four meets in your studio apartment to come up with a sales strategy, you'll naturally have something fun like pizza and beer as refreshments. When your startup is just a handful of folks trying to make something work, it goes without saying that your collective passion will be a key ingredient to your success. But once your company becomes successful and increases in size, you can't honestly expect to maintain that level of energy, creativity, and *esprit de corps.* Or can you?

Apparently, some companies think you can. At an AllThingsD conference in 2011, Apple cofounder and then-CEO Steve Jobs characterized his company's corporate culture as being "like a startup." This seems like a rather surprising assertion, given that Apple employs over 35,000 people and is currently the most valuable company in the world. In a piece for *Bloomberg Business News*, Nilofer Merchant questioned how Jobs could make such a claim, concluding that Jobs wasn't just being nostalgic: The ongoing adherence to the startup ethos was at the core of Apple's success. "The essence of what causes Apple to win," Merchant argues, "is the same thing that causes startups to innovate, the same thing that is at the root of all high-performance cultures." Steve Jobs's efforts to eliminate passive-aggressive behavior in the workplace and to encourage debates around new ideas have both been fundamental to the "smart collaboration" that fuels innovation at Apple and has come to define the company's culture.[48]

There are many examples of high-profile companies that have become successful largely due to their strong corporate culture and values. One such company that I particularly admire is Zappos, which has become the largest online shoe company since its founding just over a decade ago in 1999. Zappos posts the ten core values of its corporate culture on its website. They're all great, but one is particularly telling. The third Zappos value is to "Create fun and a little weirdness." While that may sound a bit tongue-in-cheek, the folks at Zappos mean it quite seriously. Their website explains the reasoning behind this value and the benefits of being weird as follows:

> One of the side effects of encouraging weirdness is that it encourages people to think outside the box and be more innovative. When you combine a little weirdness with making sure everyone is also having fun at work, it ends up being a win-win for everyone: Employees are more engaged in the work that they do, and the company as a whole becomes more innovative.[49]

This value really resonated with me. I've noticed the same principle in action and can attest that encouraging a fun and creative atmosphere in my own companies has brought about overwhelmingly positive results. The fact that this is a core value shows, for me at least, just how determined Zappos is to try to retain the essence of that classic startup culture, and just how beneficial such elements of the startup ethos can be to a growing company.

There's no question that the ambience and the workplace atmosphere of your startup will change as your company grows. And I'm not suggesting that a footloose, frisbee-flying environment is the best, or the only, kind of workplace to have. What I am arguing is that there is a great deal of value in the cooperative, collaborative, sometimes wacky, not-so-buttoned-down startup environment, and that you don't necessarily have to stifle or phase out these tendencies as your company becomes larger and more successful. In fact, as Zappos, Amazon, Apple, and others have shown us, fostering the very same playful yet productive "We're all in this together" spirit could very well be the reason your young upstart company grows up to be a major industry player.

BEING A GOOD CHAPERONE

While talking with an entrepreneur acquaintance recently, we started to debate when the culture of a startup first emerges. She argued that a startup needs at least 15 employees before it can amass enough personalities and stories to fully articulate the corporate culture. I had to disagree. My position is that a company's workplace culture is rooted from the beginning in the attitudes of the cofounders and evolves incrementally with each additional hire. With each new hire, it can either move toward or away from the initial core values. But the cofounders play an essential role in setting the cultural tone and leading by example. Enthusiastic cofounders usually beget enthusiastic employees. Similarly, promoting transparency from the top down has a ripple effect throughout the company and becomes one of the values. So it's a given that the way you conduct yourself will have a lot to do with your company's "personality."

The sooner your company's culture is clearly defined and clarified, the easier time you'll have in determining the cultural fit of future hires. Among your most important roles as a leader involves getting the right people on the bus and the wrong people off the bus as quickly and efficiently as possible. In fact, I liken it to being the chaperone on a school field trip. You may not be driving the bus *per se*, but you are responsible for the bus driver and all of the passengers, and you tell the driver where to go. You're obliged to set a good example by staying in your seat, not distracting the driver, and so on. And if there's a troublemaker upsetting the bus, you must swiftly deal with them, perhaps ejecting them from the bus if necessary.

So it goes for company culture. As company founder, you must set the tone in your workplace. Likewise, you must create and maintain the conditions conducive to building a strong culture. Ultimately, you will be acting as the guardian of your company's fledgling culture until it has firmly taken root. Once your company is big enough, this task becomes a team exercise in continually reinforcing and refining the company culture under the guidance of leadership.

PUT THE "CULT" IN CORPORATE CULTURE

One of the biggest things I underestimated when I started my first company over 10 years ago was the importance of corporate culture. In fact, underestimated is the wrong word—quite honestly, I didn't even recognize it as something that needed considering! It took seven years as a startup CEO before I really appreciated corporate culture, and now I'm a huge proponent of having a strong culture. Your startup's corporate culture begins to develop on Day One and needs to be consciously nurtured, both continuously and indefinitely. Much of this depends on your leadership and the example you set, but it also has to do with the people you hire and the type of atmosphere you create and promote.

Strengthening the corporate culture is now my most important responsibility as a CEO. Why? Corporate culture is the only sustainable competitive advantage over which a startup has complete control. It really is. Think about it: What other factors in business can you control? The market? Nope. The economy? No way. Tsunamis or civil war? Not a chance. Corporate culture? Yes, most definitely!

How do you define a great corporate culture? First, you need to designate the values that will form the foundation of your company culture, as well as the most important personality traits and attributes that every employee should possess. We decided on the core values of *good work*, *good people*, and *good pay*. *Good pay* is pretty straightforward—our employees should be fairly compensated with above-average wages and excellent benefits. *Good work* means work that is fun, interesting, and challenging. *Good people* are folks who have a positive attitude, are industrious and self-starting, and who are supportive of their coworkers.

Positive, *self-starting*, and *supportive* are the behavioral attributes that help us best assess the cultural fit of potential new hires, as well as serving as the yardstick against which we measure employee performance. Think of values as the non-negotiable rules of the road by which everybody at your company must abide. The desired behavioral attributes are the characteristics that a person needs to have in order to succeed and flourish at your company.

Once you've defined these core values and personality attributes, you must begin to build them into the regular rhythms of your workplace. For example, we touch on the *positive*, *self-starting*, and *supportive* cornerstones either directly or indirectly at every weekly meeting and quarterly performance review (in which these actually comprise questions that must be answered with specific examples). We have a monthly "hero" award for the employee that most personifies these attributes, as nominated by another team member. These rituals reinforce our company culture by highlighting its defining values in a variety of workplace contexts. Whatever aspect of the office you look at, the values are always there.

We also empower employees to own the culture. While the core values and attributes must stay the same, there is flexibility in how those values can be expressed and interpreted. We encourage input from employees at all levels to help us shape and sustain our company culture. For example, we require unanimous approval for any new hires; that is, any team member involved in the hiring process can veto a particular candidate, and that candidate will not move to the next round. Sometimes this takes a bit longer, but we have found that it is very effective in helping us hire outstanding people who exhibit the best cultural fit for our workplace. We also like to solicit employee feedback by way of anonymous quarterly surveys that ask if the company is living up to our core values (last quarter we had 100% somewhat agree or strongly agree; typically we get a 92%+ rate of agreement). The surveys also ask about the ultimate indicator of employee satisfaction: *How likely are you to recommend this to friends as a good place to work?* The resulting answers, along with other measured indicators like employee turnover (we typically have less than 3% turnover each year), give us a more complete picture of how well we're fulfilling our commitment to our core values.

Finally, make sure you codify and document your culture and values. We have a culture book with stories and anecdotes that explain why things are the way they are around the office, why we do things the way we do, where certain traditions came from, and so on. The book is always growing, and it has been a spectacular resource for new hires, who can browse the book and quickly familiarize themselves with our corporate culture. As people establish themselves at the company, they are encouraged to make their own submissions to the culture book. We feel that, aside from being a good teambuilding activity and shared resource, the culture book is a fun way to document the growth and evolution of the company.

THE BENEVOLENT CULT LEADER

There's a reason that the word culture starts off with "cult." Thinking of your own startup's company culture as a cult might sound strange, but it's a helpful metaphor. Many of the most famous corporate cultures have been described as "cult-like" (e.g., Zappos). When I did a summer internship at IBM after my freshman year at Duke, there was another intern there from Northwestern who kept saying she wanted to work at the SAS Institute. I asked her why, and she replied that people love it and never want to leave. That wasn't very convincing, so I asked why again. She finally admitted that it was more or less a cult she wanted to join. True story.

So am I telling you to go out and establish a cult that happens to be a profitable company? Of course not. But don't make the mistake I did as a first-time entrepreneur and underestimate your own role in setting the right tone for a strong corporate culture to flourish. Yes, having a great office with free food and drinks and fun toys like Razor Scooters and a Segway may help set the tone, but these things aren't nearly as important as establishing the right expectations and atmosphere around your office. You should also ensure that employees are properly motivated to buy in to the company culture. All of these things come from the top, so this will be one of your greatest responsibilities.

In his book *Drive: The Surprising Truth About What Motivates Us,* workplace analyst and author Dan Pink identifies three key motivational factors for employees: autonomy, mastery, and purpose. *Autonomy* means the power to choose the direction of our own lives; *mastery* relates to improving on skills that allow us to make meaningful contributions; and *purpose* involves belonging to something bigger than ourselves. John Bogle, probably best known as the founder and former CEO of the well-known Vanguard Group, explores three similar factors—autonomy, connectedness, and competence—in his book *Enough: True Measures of Money, Business, and Life*. I think all of these are important motivators, but I prefer my own combination of motivational values: autonomy, camaraderie, and mastery.

AUTONOMY, CAMARADERIE, MASTERY

Here's how I would describe the three keys to building a productive workplace and a strong corporate culture (not to mention cultivating your own personal happiness):

Autonomy

Empowering team members to make their own decisions and to have some freedom and control over the work they do, and the way they do that work, can have a powerful influence on corporate culture. This may mean letting people work saner hours (e.g., no more implied expectations of a 50+ hour work week), or allowing flexible or family-friendly schedules. After all, it's not about the actual number of hours worked, but the work that gets done, isn't it? Research has shown that being given even the most nominal ability to determine our own working conditions significantly increases our job satisfaction and loyalty. We have a "no vacation tracking" policy—we don't keep track of vacation time, and people can take it whenever they want, so long as they do so responsibly. It might sound surprising, but it's a fact that since we adopted it, nobody has ever abused this policy. To do so would go against our company culture and values, so people are reasonable in adhering to the policy. The bottom line is, when employees are treated like adults, they usually make responsible decisions.

Camaraderie

Knowing that other folks in the company (especially managers and direct reports) care about each team member on a personal level can add an important dimension of security and comfort to our workplace lives. When we know that we are perceived as people with individual needs and problems, rather than as mere functionaries or cogs in the corporate wheel, we are likely to respect others in return. Treating the company like an extended family encourages employees to interact in a spirit of cooperation rather than competition. It's all about what we can achieve as a team, rather than who can climb to the top of the ladder first. My experience has shown me that people who have fun together also work better together. Camaraderie can be fostered through team activities, fun outings and events that often include family members, and volunteer projects that also connect to the wider community. We do all three of these things at my companies. You'd be hard-pressed to find anybody in the office who doesn't enjoy hanging out with their coworkers; in fact, this is a regular occurrence for many of them, even outside of work. It's hard to revert to bickering and petty inter-office politics when everybody equates helping out your coworker with giving a friend a hand.

Mastery

My conception of mastery involves not just mastering but truly excelling at your given role, thereby achieving a level of confidence and proficiency of which you can be proud. A corporate culture that offers employees opportunities for ongoing education and chances to expand their competencies and skill sets, even if those opportunities are not always directly or specifically related to job descriptions, sends a compelling message. It says that the company values your personal growth and wants you, as an individual, to succeed at reaching your own goals. I believe that most of us relish a challenge, but also that we want a sense of purpose. That feeling of purpose and sense of mastery also comes from having a clear sense of how our own work fits into, and adds value to, the overall activities of the team and the progress of the company as a whole. As leader of your company, another crucial responsibility you have is to ensure that each employee understands how their contributions fit into the big picture and how much the company appreciates the special skills and abilities that they bring to the table.

I agree wholeheartedly with Richard Branson's observation that employees come before shareholders, customers, and vendors. As the head of a company, one of the most crucial things you can do to ensure its success is to set the right tone so that a strong corporate culture will develop around your chosen values. Everybody's motivational trinity will be different, though, so try to develop your own after giving some serious thought to the top three factors you feel will motivate your employees to excel.

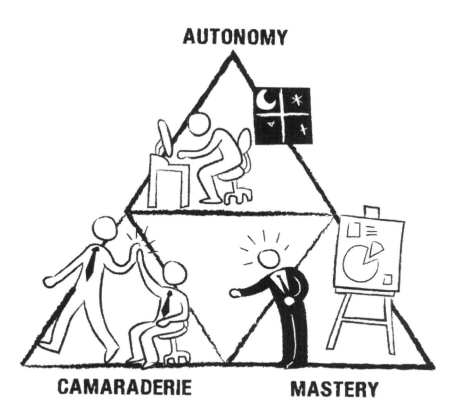

AUTONOMY

CAMARADERIE   **MASTERY**

MAKING IT HAPPEN

It's all well and good for me to go on about values and motivation and setting the tone, but when it really comes down to it, what comprises the nuts and bolts of corporate culture? As I said at the beginning of the chapter, you can think of corporate culture as a collection of workplace values, symbols, behaviors, and practices. The following section outlines some of the most established rituals and traditions that are part of our company culture.

Breaking Bread as a Team

For the first six years at my company, we recognized birthdays or a big customer win by taking the whole office out to lunch to celebrate as a team. After a while, this became such a frequent occurrence (and we had grown so much as a team) that I decided to have catered lunches delivered to our office every Friday, 52 weeks a year. We've been doing this for five years running, and it is one of the best things we do to foster employee interaction and goodwill. Here are a few reasons why we find it so beneficial:

- We do it on Fridays, giving everyone a chance to end the work week on a good note and talk about what's going on in their lives. Plans for the upcoming weekend are a popular topic of discussion.

- Breaking bread with team members is a great way to get to know each other on a more personal level, leading to stronger relationships and more trust.

- We encourage team members to bring in their spouses or kids, creating a family atmosphere.

- People love the free food no matter where it comes from, but everybody has their favorites, so there's plenty of friendly debate about which places are best to order from. We usually rotate between a few different types of food (pizza, Asian takeout, sub sandwiches, burritos), and we change up the restaurants every quarter, based on employee feedback.

I didn't know how successful this idea would be when we started, but "Free Food Fridays" have been such a hit that we now also provide free catered hot breakfast every Monday morning, in addition to simpler breakfast spreads every other day of the week. The Monday morning breakfast gives employees a chance to ease into a new work week while chatting with each other about their weekends. Humans *are* social animals, after all, so it's not too surprising that nothing makes our employees feel more like family than sharing a meal together. And instead of the old "Monday blahs" that are so widespread in many workplaces, our employees really look forward to walking into the office on a Monday morning, where they'll find a hot breakfast and chatty coworkers to help start their week on an upbeat note.

The idea of sharing meals with coworkers has become a popular one, and for the last few years running we've had an office-wide Thanksgiving potluck. This family-style event brings amateur chefs out of the woodwork, much to the delight of their hungry coworkers. It has become enough of a tradition that people eagerly anticipate the same signature dishes each year from certain team members, much in the same way family members look forward to grandma's famous pumpkin pie every Thanksgiving. It's a nice way of sharing a meal as a team at a particularly festive time of year.

As another way of bonding over a meal, we also do monthly cross-functional lunches, wherein one person from each department (Engineering, Sales, Marketing, Operations, and so on) is invited to attend an offsite lunch with me. The idea, again, is to break bread as a team, but cross-functional lunches are great in that they also allow folks who don't usually work together to interact with each other over good food and conversation. This ritual has succeeded at getting people to interact with each other across departments, which tend to become insular or cloistered when left to their own devices. As a CEO, I also really appreciate the one-on-one time I get with these small groups and the range of perspectives they share during our lunchtime chats.

In the spirit of the successful cross-functional lunches, I've started making a habit of periodically taking the most recent crop of hires out to lunch within their first month of starting. Each new hire lunch gives me a chance to interact with our newest employees in a casual setting and also allows them to get to know each other as a cohort of peers who were hired around the same time (like a "class" of new hires). Aside from the standard questions about people's backgrounds, I make a point to ask the new hires how our corporate culture and work atmosphere differ from those of their previous employer. The newbies usually give a variety of answers, but there are definitely some recurring themes in their observations:

- Our employees genuinely love coming to work every day and are passionate about the work they do.

- Our training, much of which is peer-based, is comprehensive and more hands-on and user-friendly than at other companies.

- People genuinely want to help each other succeed (e.g., sales reps don't expect a split commission when they help someone else make a sale).

- There's less arbitrary pressure to get new product features out the door and more of an emphasis on excelling at what we already do while always looking for ways to improve.

- The office atmosphere is more relaxed and casual than they've ever experienced, yet employees seem much more productive than at most other companies. (This comes as a genuine surprise to some.)

- Coworkers are friends with one another and frequently hang out after work.

Heroes and Hassles

Everybody's familiar with the time-tested idea of a suggestion box. But how do you simultaneously solicit employee feedback while also recognizing other employees for coming up with solutions?

We've found the answer in the form of our Heroes and Hassles awards. Every month, employees are encouraged to nominate internal "heroes" who have gone above and beyond to solve a problem, help a coworker, or please a client. We also solicit feedback and suggestions on issues or problems ("hassles") that need solutions. The Hero and Hassle of the month are chosen by way of direct voting through an idea exchange by coworkers; the Hero and Hassle with the most votes at the end of the month are announced as the winners at our all-hands meeting. Each winner gets a $100 bill and a kitschy lawn ornament to display on their desk as an outward symbol of their accolade. We use a free online tool (UserVoice) to keep track of nominations and to count votes, and we simply close the entries out each month to make way for new nominations the following month. Here are some key benefits we've realized from adopting this approach:

- Employee recognition is carried out in a consistent and company-wide fashion.

- The awards manage to keep their grassroots character because folks are nominated and voted on by their peers (as opposed to being recognized in a top-down manner by a handful of managers).

- From a "suggestion box" perspective, the Hassles have generated awesome suggestions for improvements, and the vote counts help us determine which issues are the most pressing.

- Using the idea exchange offers us a great way to

document unresolved problems and possible solutions and lets us return to these in the future if needed.

- Departments and team members talk about the nominations and ideas on a daily basis at our morning check-ins.

- The lawn ornament prize is a visible symbol of the winning employee's contribution and serves as an ongoing reminder to the rest of the office.

Our Hero and Hassle awards recognize employee contributions, foster communication, and help us to capture good ideas in a systematic fashion. They also demonstrate to employees that we truly want their feedback and opinions, and that their input can directly bring about change. We've found idea exchanges provide the ideal medium for this activity, but you may find other ways of doing some of the same things that are better suited to your company. The suggestion box principle is scalable and can work for even the smallest startup.

Sharing is Caring

We have all heard the saying that it is better to over-communicate than to under-communicate. One of the dynamics that has been proven to me time and time again is that, absent information, people will make up ideas to fill the void. This tendency isn't usually malicious—it's just human nature. In order to ensure transparency, employees need to feel up to date on everything that's going on, even if it's just in the form of quick summaries or brief check-ins. For this, I suggest that entrepreneurs adopt a multi-modal communication strategy including a variety of communication channels—periodic check-ins, all-hands meetings, department briefings, concise emails, and more casual exchanges at breakfast, lunch, and dinner meetings. It's a given that most people don't really enjoy meetings. But when the meetings are short, frequent, and routine—or when they take place over a pleasant meal—they become more like everyday habits and less like onerous chores. I'm a big fan of morning stand-up scrums, a type of daily check-in we use here in the office to kick off the workday. For starters, having everyone stand up and talk in front of their colleagues first thing in the morning gets energy levels up. Everyone says hello or good morning, enhancing the team's camaraderie. And because everyone hears what everybody else is up to at the start of the day, there are plenty of chances to offer each other assistance or possible solutions, either during the stand-up or as the day goes on. Finally, because the team's manager has gotten a morning briefing from all team members, if an issue comes up later in the day related to one of someone's daily priorities, it doesn't take as much time for the manager to get up to speed on something they might need help with, or vice-versa.

To reiterate, too much communication is vastly preferable to not enough communication. Remember to control your message, and don't let rumors or false information fill the gaps. It's important to not only remove the barriers to communication in the workplace, so that you get active feedback from all directions, but also to put some mechanisms in place that show that you are actively soliciting the team's voices and ideas.

Celebrating the Small Victories

When a startup first takes off, there are so many things changing on a daily basis that it's easy for entrepreneurs to spend all their time putting out fires, only being reactive to what's going on in the company. When you're caught up in the whirlwind of upcoming releases, new clients, and an expanding staff, you tend to overlook the small stuff. But it's important to stop and smell the roses once in a while, so to speak.

Celebrating those oft-ignored small victories helps you put things in perspective. (I'm talking about minor but genuine wins, as opposed to the more formal signed-on-the-dotted line sort of victories.) Sure, you might have to take care of some outstanding bug fixes before your product will function optimally, but when a delighted customer mentions that product's amazing new feature on Twitter, there's still reason to celebrate. We also make a point to regularly share snippets of positive feedback on our product and customer service, straight from client messages, via company-wide emails. The steady stream of compliments and the ensuing congratulatory comments really keep people in good spirits and help us maintain a positive atmosphere in which employees can be applauded for making even the most minor contribution.

As great as the positive feedback emails have been for us, I've come to realize that there are times when you should just stop everything, gather the team together, and do some cheerleading. As easy as technologies like instant messaging, Skype, and email have made it to avoid doing things in person, nothing beats the emotional connection of being face-to-face with your employees. And celebrating those victories spontaneously, immediately after they happen (rather than months later at the next performance review), can have profound, far-reaching effects on morale at all levels of the organization.

In our office, we like to have sales reps ring a gong as soon as they close a deal. This lets everybody know that a small victory just happened, and among those employees who actually witness the gonging, the celebratory spirit is palpable. We also have in-office happy hours on the last Friday of every month to encourage employee interaction and to show everyone appreciation for another month of great work. But whether the events are for general appreciation or specific recognition, they all encourage an atmosphere of excitement over shared achievements. I can say with certainty that our corporate culture has flourished in large part because we consistently celebrate even the smallest of victories in a variety of ways.

Connecting With the Community

One way we foster team camaraderie while simultaneously giving back to the world outside our office is through our 1% community service time policy. What this means is that all employees are allowed, at the expense of the company, to spend 1% of their working hours volunteering in the community with a local organization or nonprofit. Given the standard 40-hour work week for a 50-week year, the average employee works for 2,000 hours, of which 1% (20 hours, or 2.5 workdays) can be dedicated solely to offsite community service. Typically we set up a half-day service project, solicit employee participation by way of signups, and then go together as a group to complete the activity (which is treated as though it was half of a regular workday). It's an optional program, but most of our team members participate in at least one of these projects. Some of the community service projects we have undertaken so far include:

- Participating in mentoring days for the Boys & Girls Club and Junior Achievement
- Spearheading a cleanup effort in a local neighborhood park
- Preparing a special meal for cancer patients at a local hospice
- Working on natural resource conservation with the Piedmont Park Conservancy

Beyond the obvious benefits of doing good in our local community, we have found that community service projects provide great teambuilding opportunities that build rapport both within and across departments and boost overall morale as well.

Not least is the fact that these projects really do help all of us keep things in perspective. As your own company grows, you will have many opportunities to establish that your company culture recognizes its commitment and connection to the community. But as the example of our 1% program shows, even the smallest startups can send the message that they value their community connections. These are just a few ideas that have been especially successful for us. You'll establish your own traditions with input from your employees over time. Putting policies like this one in place is an excellent way to help your company culture take hold.

CORPORATE CULTURE STARTS WITH YOU

As the founder of your startup, everything starts with you. If your mission statement, vision statement, marketing message, or pretty much any of your actions as a leader don't align with your stated values, the corporate culture will necessarily suffer. If you're too busy to make time for employee interaction, too distracted to listen to problems, or too lenient with disciplining or removing those who are set on creating toxic company politics, then your company culture will seem like a sham. Doling out rewards to a few favored individuals while singing the praises of teamwork only casts your value set as a bunch of hollow platitudes. No matter how you go about it, be sure that you maintain consistency between what you say and what you do.

As much as your company's culture depends on cues from leadership, it is not an entirely top-down process. Corporate culture must also be organic in its development. People really have to believe in your company values, and they must truly want to belong to your organization. You need buy-in from employees for the company's culture to take root and grow. Otherwise, you'll be engaging in yet another pointless upper management exercise that doesn't translate to anything substantial where it matters most: in the trenches.

A healthy, productive corporate culture doesn't just happen. It develops over time and with dedication out of the highly conscious actions of and the examples set by leaders and management. And don't assume that corporate culture doesn't affect the bottom line; there have been many studies with results showing the contrary.[50] The businesses on *Fortune Magazine's* "100 Best Companies to Work For" list also happen to be among the most profitable ones. This relationship is not one of chance. It is a direct result of the powerful effects that a strong corporate culture has on the success and profitability of a business.

Creating a strong corporate culture is hard work, and it's an ongoing challenge. But it's also fun and rewarding. Most of all, it's crucial to your startup's success, because corporate culture is the only sustainable competitive advantage that's totally within your control.

CHAPTER 12 ■ GROWTH IS GREAT…NOW WHAT?

Growth: It's one of those things that every entrepreneur dreams of achieving, from the time the first idea is scribbled down on a napkin. But growth is a funny thing. You find yourself wishing for it, breaking your back and beating your brain in the hopes that soon your startup will take off as it begins to experience real growth. As soon as you've finally reached that goal, part of you wonders what you've gotten yourself into as you quickly realize that growth carries with it a unique set of issues and challenges that you weren't expecting.

In order to get a good handle on growth and its challenges, it's helpful to begin by sketching out the various stages through which a typical startup progresses. Not all startups progress at the same rate, and sometimes stages can be unusually short or extremely long. For example, the concept stage, or "napkin stage" as we referred to it in earlier chapters, can become significantly protracted if you run into issues and have to change your product or approach. As you learn more and your idea evolves, your startup concept can change, sometimes completely. But regardless of the length of time you spend in each stage or the unique aspects of your own company's experience, it will follow a trajectory of growth common to all startups.

THE STAGES OF A STARTUP

A frequently cited business metaphor describes the lack of agility in big companies in watercraft terms: A big company is like a tanker ship that has immense momentum but little ability to change course. I prefer to think of it as a cruise ship. There's a lot of value aboard, and while the ride is enjoyable, your preplanned route doesn't allow for last-minute detours. Let's take the boat analogy a bit further and apply it to the many stages of a startup.

Concept Stage
You've spent many hours researching your options and have finally

settled on the boat of your dreams. You know what you want your dream boat to look like. You imagine countless scenarios about how you'll operate it and where you'll take it—and how awesome it will be—but it's still just a dream. And at the moment, the reality is that you're just getting used to navigating your starter watercraft, a basic **rowboat.** Rowing is hard work, and sometimes it seems like all you do is paddle upstream. But the ride is gratifying, and you're starting to really get into this whole boat thing. You've got another boating fanatic on board (your cofounder), which lightens the burden of constantly rowing the boat and navigating through rapids.

Seed Stage

You realize that, despite doing your homework, you can't really afford the boat of your dreams (at least not right now). But your skills have improved and you really want to get out on the water, so you and your cofounder figure you'll take turns riding a **jet ski.** You thought it wouldn't be too exciting, but you quickly find yourself musing, *Wow, this thing goes fast! And it turns on a dime!* While the jet ski isn't exactly what you pictured yourself riding, you can't deny that it's thrilling to zip around the lake at top speed. You find the ride exhilarating, exhausting, and a bit disorienting...but you can't wait to go again.

Early Stage

Okay, now you have a few more people who want to hang out with you and your water-loving cofounder. They all agree to pitch in to help maintain and run the boat, and maybe to kick in some money for gas and upkeep. So you decide that it's time you upgraded to a larger, better equipped **motorboat**—maybe something like a MasterCraft with an in-board motor that's able to go fast and turn hard. This robust boat gets the job done, but it's still agile enough to change course relatively quickly. Plus, you can afford a few bells and whistles, so your boat looks pretty snazzy too. For thrill-seekers, this can be the most exciting stage.

Growth Stage

Things on your little boat are starting to get a bit crowded. You need a bigger crew and more space to accommodate them. (People have started demanding decent sleeping quarters!) Looks like it's time to splurge on the 50' Hatteras **yacht.**

You consider that you'll have to slow things down somewhat and be more deliberate with your navigation, but your growing pains make a bigger boat a necessary next step. Plus, having a yacht will be pretty

sweet. Just think of all the interesting places you can take it and the awesome parties you can throw on it. You conclude that giving up a bit of flexibility is well worth the benefits that come along with having a high-performance luxury craft.

Late Stage

Your party has begun to overflow the confines of your 50' yacht. With so much already invested and the growth showing no signs of stopping, you realize you're going to need a cruise ship. Before long, you've left the port to set sail on the open ocean. It's a little scary out there, but it's exciting, and you can't wait to see where it'll take you. Plus, you're still having lots of fun. And while there's a ton of value on board, you must resign yourself to the fact that changing course is pretty difficult. Your route is planned out long in advance, and you can't make the kind of impulsive changes you used to with your smaller, more agile crafts. You must stay the course and stick to the itinerary for the most part.

Maybe you've aimed high with your dreams, planning for a future when your company is pumped to the brim with venture capital so that it becomes a behemoth worth hundreds of millions of dollars, just like that high-value cruise ship. Maybe you want to develop a product in the hopes that an industry leader like Google or Facebook will acquire your company for a few million bucks a couple of years down the road. Or maybe you're aiming for a lifestyle business—something with the revenue predictability that gives you the freedom to make rewarding life choices and take great vacations. But no matter the size of the dream, everybody wants their startup to grow, and everyone envisions it succeeding.

ENDURING GROWING PAINS

Fast growth in a startup is the proverbial "nice problem to have," but rapid or unexpected growth has meant the demise of more than a few promising companies. It's not good to over-anticipate growth, mostly because that means putting money into resources that you don't need just yet. But letting growth catch you totally by surprise can put you in a similarly tough position, leaving chaos in its wake. There are plenty of pitfalls to watch out for during the growth stage, but below are the areas where you're likely to feel the most serious growing pains.

Staffing

It's inevitable that hiring will accelerate as you hit a growth spurt. Up until that point, you were probably pretty careful about hires, recruiting slowly and intelligently and interviewing carefully (using Topgrading techniques, I hope), and really putting in the time to fully train and support those new hires. But when the growth spurt hits, the need to staff up quickly can put pressure on those standards, causing you to turn a blind eye to inadequate skill sets, to get lazy about checking references and running background checks, and (perhaps worst of all) to leave new folks adrift on an unfamiliar and turbulent sea. The growth stage will naturally require you to expand your hiring, and it's also the obvious time for rounding out the skill sets and areas of expertise in which your startup is lacking. But merely throwing new hires into the mix without assigning clear roles, responsibilities, and reporting structures is both counterproductive and expensive. Turnover rates might increase, and that unwritten business adage, "Never enough time to do it right, but always enough time to do it over," will catch up to you before you know it. You might be able to manage, at least for a while, without a full-fledged human resources person or department, but eventually you will have to put some variation of a management layer in place. In a situation like this (probably a pretty likely scenario), every human resource process (written policies, employee reviews, salary scales, etc.) that you've already documented—so long as it also conforms to your corporate culture—will put you far ahead of the game.

Customer Support

One of the first threads to snap in periods of rapid growth, assuming your servers don't go down, involves the quality of customer support. It goes without saying that if you expand too quickly, taking on too many new customers before you can catch up with staffing needs, then the quality of your customer service will suffer. It's damage you can't afford to weather. To guard against a customer service breakdown, startups should put as much effort into understanding and addressing support calls as they do into growth, as the two go hand in hand. Uncovering and fixing customer support issues will enable your company to grow steadily, without excessive spending and without an overwhelmed support team. The online resources you offer, such as a knowledge base, user guides, FAQs, and user forums should be built out to be as comprehensive as possible, preferably *before* you experience rapid growth; likewise, you need to put tested training mechanisms in place ahead of time to ensure that you have capable and prepared customer support personnel.

Communication & Transparency

When there are only two or three of you in your startup, office communication is easy. You just walk over (or swivel your chair) and talk to each other, right? However, as your company grows, particularly if that growth is rapid, communication becomes exponentially more challenging. Communication channels and decision paths must be formalized and routine procedures established. Meetings will necessarily have to become more regular and more structured; you can't just keep running over to Starbucks together whenever you need to discuss something of consequence. And somebody—or maybe several somebodies—will have to assume responsibility for knowing where information should go and for seeing that it reaches its destination (hence, the appearance of middle management and the dreaded Org Chart). One of the biggest challenges faced by a business in a stage of high growth is the task of managing communication, and doing it efficiently. Companies that don't scale up their communication processes will certainly run into business-side difficulties, but they will also discover that morale and corporate culture are adversely affected by insufficient or dysfunctional communication.

I've already made my point about team members filling in the blanks with gossip in the absence of real information, but this kind of speculation can also run wild among your customers and social media followers. Be as transparent as possible both internally and externally. Keep your followers and visitors up to date about what's going on with the company, and they'll be as empathetic with your growing pains as they were with your birth pangs. Emailing, tweeting, or blogging about your company's latest developments and news items will fill in that information vacuum, both informing and reassuring your loyal tribe.

Cash Management

A period of rapid expansion and the resulting revenue that comes in can bring welcome relief from cash stressors, particularly for the bootstrapping entrepreneur. There's a temptation to bulk up expense accounts, adjust salaries, spread out into new offices, or acquire fancy equipment. Some of these things may actually be feasible, so this is certainly a good time for you to review your budgets. It's also appropriate for you to start thinking about preserving and securing some capital assets for the company's future, not to mention your own.

But don't succumb to the temptation to "grow out of" your scrappy mindset. Now's not the time to stop controlling expenses or to throw budget constraints out the window. For technology startups especially, growth rarely occurs in a linear fashion. While it's not unusual that you might, in the back of your mind, genuinely want to believe that you've hit Facebook-style exponential growth, the reality is that growth patterns are normally cyclical, and you'll need cash for that next acceleration.

THE CEO TRANSITION

Most entrepreneurs dream about one day getting to take the helm of that Hatteras yacht, or even wearing the ultimate captain's hat while piloting that huge, powerful cruise ship. But when it actually happens, many of them discover that they're pretty uncomfortable. As a startup founder, you've gotten used to having your hand in every pie, wearing every conceivable hat, knowing the details of every operation, and making most of the decisions that determine the direction of the company. But as a company gets larger, the time comes when it simply cannot be micromanaged any longer. Trying to continue doing everything as you always have won't accomplish anything but stunting the company's growth. Up until this point, your management style has probably been primarily reactive, highly individualistic, and often intuitive. But what your company needs now is a proactive, strategic, and forward-looking leader.

Many founders have trouble letting go. The loss of control, whether perceived or actual, can be brutally hard on the ego and can terrify control freaks. When it becomes clear that what was once a fun game has suddenly turned serious, the weight of each decision can be crushing. In fact, some founders leave of their own accord in the growth stage, cashing out or hiring their replacements.

Ironically, the kind of personality traits and the skill set that best serve a startup do not necessarily remain the same when you decide to take the company to the next level. Growing awareness of that fact can cause internal friction for the founder, strife between cofounders, trouble between cofounders and the board, or some nightmarish combination of these. Publishing company Wiley Technology is a case in point. After founder Lew Cirne developed Wiley's core technology, made some big sales, and landed several key clients, ultimately spearheading a strategic transformation of the company, the board actually asked him to resign! After getting past the initial shock, Cirne agreed and subsequently became involved in finding his own replacement. He had come to the realization that "the world's best speedboat captain isn't able to pilot an oil tanker."[51]

But this is not to say that making the successful transition from a small startup's entrepreneur-founder to the CEO of a big company can't be done. Microsoft, HP, Wal-Mart, FedEx, Siebel, Dell, Disney,

Starbucks, Motorola, and Sony are just a few of the companies in which the founders were able to make that transition. Still, it's true that the necessary change in management style that such a transition requires can be pervasive and uncomfortable, especially if you're the type of founder who simply can't imagine other people piloting the same ship you worked so hard on to make seaworthy in the first place. Before you encounter the classic "nice problem to have," it's not a bad idea to be aware of some of the challenges that the company's growth might bring, not just from an operational standpoint, but for you personally.

KNOWING WHEN TO EXPAND

Lance Weatherby, a serial entrepreneur and former startup catalyst at Georgia Tech, has done a great job of describing the growth stage in his blog, *Force of Good*. The key characteristic of the growth stage is that revenue is accelerating for the startup. The revenue curve—the classic hockey stick—becomes steeper up to a point, at which time the rate slows, indicating that the company has matured beyond the startup stage. Funding for the growth stage can come from a range of equity sources: venture capital firms, private equity funds, or, if you're bootstrapping, from profits.[52]

The serious challenge for the bootstrapped startup is determining exactly *when* to expand. There's a fine line between maintaining sufficient reserves in the bank and being suitably aggressive with new hires and new initiatives. Five years ago, after struggling with this issue for over a year and experimenting with different ideas, I settled on an approach I've been using ever since. I have dubbed this as the *Growth Plan Assets* (GPA) metric.

The GPA, much like a college GPA, is expressed in simplified form as a number that summarizes the ratio of current assets to the company's average monthly operating costs over the previous 90 days. The GPA is a measure of how many months you can continue to operate normally without bringing in any additional revenues. Used as a metric, it tells you at a glance whether or not your business is ready to expand. Here's how I calculate it:

1. Add up all current assets, including cash in the bank and accounts receivable that are not overdue.

2. Calculate the average monthly costs of operation of the business over the past 90 days (include every single penny you spent that wasn't a one-time cost).

3. Divide the current assets by the average monthly cost to get the GPA.

Think of the GPA like a college GPA: it's measured on a 0-4 point scale, where 4.0 is excellent, 3.0 is good, 2.0 is average, and 1.0 is borderline or failing. You know you're ready to expand when your company's GPA surpasses the standard college GPA range (2.0-3.0). So, just like the average college student, most of the time your company is going to hover somewhere in the two- or three-point range. When you start getting straight As and begin to approach a 4.0, then you know that you have a sufficient GPA to expand. The GPA is also relative to recurring revenue, such that the more recurring revenue you have, the lower the GPA threshold can be for you to expand.

Growth, when it comes, doesn't have to be wild or uncontrollable. Developing a growth strategy based on what is profitable and sustainable for your own business, and drawing up an action plan for attaining those objectives and for adjusting your operations and infrastructure to manage that growth, constitute tasks that are far less difficult than what you've already managed to accomplish. Don't let these technical exercises scare you off. Like that prototype business model thesis, those early financial models, or that first product release, the growth strategy you come up with initially isn't going to be perfect. It takes iteration to balance frugality with fast growth and scalability. But thinking ahead can prepare you for choppy waters and reduce the risks of capsizing your boat.

Making a Graceful Exit

People like to make polite conversation with entrepreneurs by asking the classic *What's your exit strategy?* question. I like to ask it too, but for a different reason: to get a feel for an entrepreneur's approach to their business. While the growth stage can last for many years, once you make it to the next level, the exit strategy question quickly moves from the theoretical to the practical. Get to here, Lance Weatherby advises, and the company has two main options: achieve liquidity through an acquisition or IPO (increasingly rare these days), or manage the business for cash flow. But, he notes, as the entrepreneur, you also have two options. You can either "return to concept stage" to redesign your offerings or build a new product, or you can simply "enjoy what you have built and continue to make it even better."[53]

STAGE LEFT

My preferred exit strategy is not to have one. When people ask about my exit strategy, I typically answer along the lines of the following: *My goal is to build the coolest, most innovative, and most profitable company possible. If an acquirer comes along, I will consider it, but my primary goal is to develop a successful company that is built to last.* You might have a difference of opinion on this question, but I truly believe that building a sustainable, enduring company is the highest form of entrepreneurship. Anyone can achieve short-term success, but it takes an exceptionally talented entrepreneur to build a legendary organization that is able to maintain its personality and character for the long haul.

CHAPTER 13 ▪ I AM NOT MY BUSINESS!

We're always talking about it, aren't we? *How do you find the ideal balance between your work and personal life?* It's a favorite interview question for celebrities, for people in powerful positions, and yes, even for entrepreneurs. *How do you manage your work/life balance?* Or, in layman's terms: How do you manage to do all this and still be a normal person?

Most people get a little off-balance at some point or another, but startup entrepreneurs are extraordinarily vulnerable to letting their work/life balance get out of whack. It's the fundamental nature of a startup to demand all of your attention all of the time, and when you want so badly for your dreams to become a reality, it's very tempting to talk yourself out of a personal life on the grounds that it's good for the business. Many of us commit our life savings, sacrifice family time, and become heavily indebted, all in the name of starting our companies. We're simply not in it alone. There are other cofounders, employees and team members, and all of their families to consider as well. Taken together, this can be a heavy burden to bear. And we take the responsibility very seriously, often believing that the only way to give evidence of our sincerity and commitment is to work, work, work. And then work some more.

Having done my time in the entrepreneurial trenches, I understand the pressure to put everything you have into your business, even at the expense of your personal life. But I can speak from experience also in offering two personal truisms: (1) Working smarter trumps working longer, and (2) I am not my business.

WORK SMARTER, NOT LONGER

When people complain about their work/life balance being off, it's usually because they are feeling overwhelmed and unable to juggle all of their responsibilities. It may feel like there's just too much work to do, and not enough time to get it all done. It is especially ironic, then, that there is so much truth in the old saying, "If you want something done, go to the busiest person you know." I think the answer to the work/life balance puzzle lies in the fact that some people just work smarter than others. They're better at planning and prioritizing and have a system that guides their work and their thinking. If you want to get it all done, instead of worrying about how you're going to make more time, start thinking of ways you can use your time more effectively and efficiently. Work smarter, not longer.

Just Do It!

People often ask me how I get so many different things done. It's true that I have a good bit going on, and like everyone, I sometimes struggle to keep up with it all. But the fact is, I move quickly and trust my intuition. I'm completely confident in my ability to read something once, make a gut decision, and never look back. Sometimes I make mistakes, but I consider them to be learning experiences. For the most part, though, this approach has served me well. Going with my gut almost always turns out well in the end, and the fact that

I make decisions without mulling over things for too long means that I save a lot of time in the end. When I find myself hesitating, I tell myself (to paraphrase Nike) *Just do it!*

Making the most of your time takes practice, but the results are well worth the effort. You essentially must train yourself to develop beneficial habits and to routinely use good time management techniques. Once these become part of your routine, they will become second nature. I follow a few simple time management guidelines of my own:

- The first thing I do when I get to the office each day is review what I accomplished the day before and then write down what I'm going to do that day, prioritizing my list items accordingly.

- I don't call unnecessary meetings or meetings without a clear objective, and I expect others to do the same. This isn't just me being a nice guy; in fact, it actually helps all of us get more done.

- I only read emails once and handle them on the spot whenever possible. And I never go to bed with an email in my inbox; I either reply immediately or move the email to a folder. Inbox Zero was hard to get to, but once I reached it, it has since been easy to maintain.

- I love delegating to people smarter than I am and watching what they produce. Most of the time I'm pleased with the outcome.

- I read at least 100 blog posts and articles a week, and I

post to my own blog on a daily basis. I get ideas for posts through conversations with colleagues and friends, things I observe in the workplace, and other topics on which I feel like reflecting. New ideas of any kind are invigorating and give me energy and direction.

I don't believe there is one right way for people to get things done. This is just a short list of methods that work for me. I need a system in place and guidelines to follow. By planning and prioritizing my daily tasks, resisting procrastination, delegating whatever I can, and refreshing my store of ideas regularly, I find that I'm more on top of things and less overburdened and out-of-balance.

Lately I have seen the 60/40 time allocation rule appear in a few different books and blog posts. The general idea is that you should spend 60% of your time doing proactive or strategic work that helps you achieve your goals, and 40% of your time doing reactive or non-strategic work, which is stuff like paperwork and responding to emails—things that you must do in order to keep your business running and to stay in touch with others. With tools at our fingertips such as continuously updated news sites, RSS feeds of popular blogs, and social networking tools like Facebook, Twitter, and LinkedIn, it's easier than ever before to accomplish your 40% (non-strategic items). Recently I've been paying more attention to my strategic (60%) time allocation by becoming more engaged with my companies' product development roadmaps, as well as by participating in activities outside the office, such as conferences and industry roundtables. Just being more cognizant of how and where I spend my time has been a great help as far my time management is concerned.

Work that *Gives* You Energy?!

Have you ever spent hours tackling a tough issue, only to realize once you've completed it that you have even more energy than when you started? Some work takes energy, some is neutral, and some actually invigorates you. One of the techniques I've been trying to use lately involves paying close attention to what sorts of things really excite me, which things are a pain, and which ones have no effect. You might have your own way of doing this, but I find that following a particular process helps me.

I keep a notebook to record everything I do that energizes me and everything I do that saps my energy. Some people prefer to use a note-taking app like Evernote on their smartphone, but I like jotting things down. I make a point to do this every day, and if you do the same, you will eventually start to see patterns and trends in your entries. Once you've identified these, ask yourself what you can do to reorganize your life in such a way that allows you to do more of the energizing projects and fewer energy-draining ones. Then, come up with a good way to compartmentalize your energy-draining projects into smaller sub-tasks, or tackle them at certain times when your energy levels are typically already low (e.g., right after lunch or at the end of the work day). This process won't work for everyone, but it works well for me.

I personally don't think boredom has a place in startups. If you're bored, you're probably doing something wrong. By contrast, if you're ecstatically exhausted, you're most likely on the right track. The very nature of a startup means that there's a never-ending supply of things to do and not enough people to execute all the great ideas you have. That's why I was surprised recently when an entrepreneur confided in me that he was bored with doing a certain necessary business task involving a third-party service. He actually used the word *bored,* but I knew what he really meant: the function in question was no longer adding any value to the business. It wasn't generating energy for him or benefits for his company. My takeaway from that conversation was that as soon as something becomes boring or doesn't add value, immediately kill it. Too much cruft crops up along the way as your business grows; leaving things in place that you don't care about only slows you down and cripples the company's growth. Most of us stick mindlessly with stale tasks and activities long after their expiration date has passed. Get in there and clear things out and you'll be surprised at how much more efficiently things will operate.

Achieving Management Zen

One of the recurring themes in the autobiography of tennis great Andre Agassi is his coach reminding him to control what he can control. There's little sense in obsessing over things that are beyond your control, but when you really focus on those things that you *do* have some power over, you will be more effective and time-efficient. It sounds pretty "zen master" of me to advocate following this line of thought, but I really do think that you should take such advice to heart. Many entrepreneurs, myself included, are perfectionists by nature and can be micromanaging control freaks at times—not really the best management style to adopt, as it only succeeds in driving people crazy. Although worrying about every little detail might come naturally to us, it usually ends up being counterproductive, and we find we've wasted our energy on things that are out of our control. The best results come when we learn to control those things we can control and to let everything else go.

What are some of the things that we *can't* control? Here are a few off the top of my head:

- Economic conditions
- Competitive market forces
- Unexpected change
- Natural disasters
- The number of hours in a day

As an entrepreneur, you'll have a lot of say, but you really can't control *everything*. It's best to accept this so you can spend your time and energy elsewhere. Most of what we worry about never ends up happening anyway. So when you catch yourself tossing and turning in the middle of the night over some anxiety or fear that is simply beyond your power, try to laugh at yourself for forgetting the zen master's advice and go back to sleep. If you find it impossible to stop worrying, at least try to focus your attention on those things that you *can* control.

Little by Little

There is a saying in Kiswahili—*haba na haba, hujaza kibaba*—which means "Little by little, you'll fill up the container." I find this bit of folk wisdom especially helpful when thinking about goal-setting. The tendency when setting goals is to dream big and set the bar extraordinarily high. After all, if you don't have ambitious targets, why bother, right? Wrong. In fact, I'd argue that the opposite is true: If you want to achieve major accomplishments, the best way to do it is to break your goals down into smaller, more manageable tasks. And how do you do this? By identifying the habits and behaviors that are necessary to realize those goals.

Let me give an example to illustrate what I mean. One of the topics discussed at a recent EO University workshop centered on building a three-year life plan. The plan incorporated three basic categories: Professional, Personal, and Family. Generally, the idea was to identify where you wanted to go and, more specifically, which *habits* you needed to begin developing in order to get there. We were given an example scenario, which I have put into a table below.

The exercise was fairly straightforward, but I found it to be very helpful. It really got me thinking not just about goals, but about the small habits we can begin working on immediately in order to achieve them. I suspect that most of us spend too much time focused on the prize while ignoring the process. The problem with aiming high in your goal-setting is that lofty goals can be intimidating and overwhelming, so much so that they can paralyze us. It's a little like dreaming of playing the piano in Carnegie Hall without taking into account all of the lessons and practice you'll have to commit to before that can happen. When you're setting your goals, it makes sense to build in all of the steps it's going to take to get there. Bit by bit, you will eventually have taken all the steps you need to reach your goal.

	Goal	Habit
Professional	Secure two annual speaking engagements	Publish one article per quarter in an industry publication
	Sell a new deal each month	Meet 100 new people every month
Personal	Run a marathon	Run three miles every other day to begin training
	Break 90 in golf	Hit range balls two times per week
Family	Have a healthy relationship with my spouse	Designate one dedicated date night per week
	Become more engaged with my children	Have dinner with the kids five nights per week

While it's fairly obvious that professional goals lend themselves well to this sort of divvying up of process into habits, it should also be noted that our personal and family lives are built from little habits as well. The great thing about the three-year life plan is that it's holistic. It includes personal and family goals, too. Of course it's important to concentrate on developing the kind of habits that bring us professional success, but we shouldn't do so at the expense of those habits that help us achieve our own personal or family goals. Also try to remember that it's not just about developing good habits—it's also about breaking bad habits. Run three miles once a month and you've gotten yourself some exercise. Do it regularly and you've started building a positive habit. Miss your wedding anniversary, a birthday party, or your kid's soccer game just once, and it's a regrettable event. Do it regularly, and you've begun building a bad habit.

I AM NOT MY BUSINESS!

Years ago someone told me an interesting story about Lee Iacocca. As president of the Chrysler Corporation, the story went, Iacocca would always ask top management candidates where they had gone for their vacation the previous year. Candidates who admitted, or even bragged, that they had not taken a vacation in the last twelve months were immediately removed from consideration. (I was told that there were a lot of these.) For

Iacocca, the thinking was that an individual who could not manage his own time and his own life well enough to take an annual vacation would also be a poor manager of the company's time and resources.

Whether this story is true or just the stuff of legend, it still illustrates an important point about maintaining a healthy work/life balance and contains a valuable lesson for entrepreneurs about setting priorities. Just remember that as an entrepreneur, you are not your business. You might've poured

"No matter what you've done for yourself or for humanity, if you can't look back on having given love and attention to your own family, what have you really accomplished?"

— **Lee Iacocca**

everything you've got—money, time, ideas, energy—into building your company, but it still doesn't define you as a person. Make sure that you're at your personal best before you can make your business the best it can be.

Value Added Time

Overburdened entrepreneurs tend to think that every single second that they're not spending on expanding their business or addressing the company's problems is a "loss" in terms of opportunities missed, potential deals not made, or milestones to success postponed. They are much less likely to consider any contribution to their own health, or to their family's or teammates' physical or emotional well-being, as a value-added proposition in terms of the clarity, energy, and focus that it might return to them—and, by extension, their business—yet it is. Even a walk, an exercise class, or time spent working out in a home gym can improve your sleep cycle, bring down your blood pressure, energize you for business and personal life, and generally make you much more pleasant at work and at play. We should all think about the time we devote to our physical and emotional self as being equivalent to value added time to the business. And that includes vacations.

Don't Sacrifice Your Life

My observation has been that, as a group, successful entrepreneurs tend to be exceptionally fortunate in being surrounded by supportive friends and families, not to mention especially tolerant and long-suffering spouses and partners. It's one of the factors in their success. But even if you're part of that lucky group, remember that those terrific human resources also have their limits. Pursuing your business goals shouldn't come at the cost of destroying your personal life.

In a much lauded column called "10 Tips for Saving Your Life from Your Business," business planning expert Tim Berry argues that those who advise entrepreneurs to build their businesses first and then build their lives are using flawed thinking:

> For every successful entrepreneur who cites sacrificing health and family as the key to success, there are 10 others who say sacrificing health and family is a tragic mistake. Another logical flaw: millions of people sacrificed health and family and weren't successful. All their sacrifice did was ruin their lives. Nobody quotes them. They call that survivor bias.[54]

I completely agree with Berry and think that it's a grave mistake to postpone "life" until the day our business goals have been reached. We can't know whether that day will come soon enough. We don't know whether we'll recognize it, much less fully acknowledge it, once it arrives. We can't be sure, based on the bad habits we've built and the good ones we've neglected, that there will be anything left to salvage. None of us want our marriages, family lives, or relationships with our kids to fall victim to our success. And besides all of this, business goals never go away completely—they just change. Every time you reach a milestone, there will be new goals looming on the horizon. Why not make that ongoing journey with some sense of stability in your home life and personal affairs?

As I said earlier, I've been there and know how hard it is. If you *didn't* sometimes get a bit unbalanced with regard to your work and your "life," you'd be the exception, rather than the rule. And I'll be the first to admit that I need to start taking my own advice more to heart. Here it is again, to recap:

- Plan and prioritize to save time and get more done. Becoming cognizant of how you spend your time is the first step in planning.

- Exploit the benefits of completing energizing tasks and working hardest at the times of day when you're most energetic.

- Build the little habits that enable you to meet holistic life goals.

- Control what you can control and let the rest go.

- Learn to think of the family vacation, time spent in the gym, and other sensible steps you must take to safeguard your own health and well-being (or your employees') as value added benefits to your business.

- Kill the cruft!

Finally, we all need to remember that while our business is a very important part of our lives, it's only one part of many. Repeat after me: *I am not my business*.

CHAPTER 14 ▪ NEED SOME HELP?

Even in the midst of the creative excitement (and chaos) of launching a startup, there will be times when most entrepreneurs will feel isolated. And there will be no shortage of times when you have no idea where to turn for advice on a pressing problem. Because your experience has been yours alone, you might feel like your company is a special case, or that your problems are individual and unique.

Fortunately, you're not alone. Almost any obstacle you could ever encounter in the course of starting a company has likewise been confronted and tackled by somebody else, or possibly lots of somebodies, before you. Plenty of other entrepreneurs have been there and done that, and they've almost certainly experienced the very same feelings and frustrations that you're having. You'll have to be a bit proactive. You might have to make a real effort to seek out and connect with a mentor, counselor, colleague, or friend who can support and advise you. But the help is out there, if you're willing to locate and utilize it. You don't have to do it alone.

THE POWER OF A MENTOR

Probably the single best thing you can do to minimize those feelings of isolation, as well as to insulate yourself against business failure in general, is to find and work with a mentor. A mentor can really be anybody, but ideally you'll want someone with significant business or life experience who is in a position to guide and advise you. Even someone with the extraordinary business acumen of Bill Gates wouldn't hesitate to admit having a mentor. (As mentors go, I expect that Warren Buffett has been a pretty good one.) But for most of us, nobody immediately comes to mind when we first start thinking about finding a mentor. Massively successful people with humble and approachable personalities like Buffett are the obvious ideal, but they're hard to come by. It's difficult to know where to begin your search, and once you've finally found a suitable candidate, it can be intimidating to actually ask for their help.

But when you really think about it, we probably shouldn't be so hesitant to approach a potential mentor for guidance. According to Kathy Kram, Professor of Organizational Behavior at Boston University and author of multiple books on professional mentoring, mentoring is a bidirectional process from which the mentor also benefits. Kram points out that, by going through the process of assisting a mentee, even the most experienced mentors acquire new skills and discover latent aptitudes.[55] So don't think of it as begging for a favor from a successful somebody who's probably too busy to bother with a nobody. Chances are, they'll be glad to have the opportunity for personal growth that goes along with sharing what they know with a less experienced neophyte. I believe that most people truly enjoy helping others and paying something forward from the successes they've achieved. I know that I do. If there's a guru in your field or within your professional circles whom you admire or emulate, you shouldn't hesitate to ask if he or she might be available for a little wisdom-sharing. The worst that can happen is that you've delivered a genuine compliment. Just remember that potential mentors, to quote Kram, "are most receptive to people who ask good questions, listen well to the responses and demonstrate that they are hungry for advice and counsel."[56]

Interacting with business veterans brings invaluable rewards to startup entrepreneurs, but most of us also benefit from other types of mentoring, so it certainly can't hurt to have more than one mentor. Having multiple mentors can provide a safety net of sorts, simply because you're getting a variety of second opinions on the issues you encounter. A mentor who is a friend or family member will be most highly vested in your success and happiness, so they're good for helping with work/life balance; they're also the best outlet for venting or when you just want a sympathetic ear.

NEVER EAT ALONE

The business bestseller *Never Eat Alone* by Keith Ferrazzi easily ranks as one of my favorite books. It's an enjoyable read, but most of all, it demonstrates the sheer power of peer networking in the business world and the value of relationship building in ensuring entrepreneurs' success. Regardless of your industry, continually establishing new relationships is a critical part of entrepreneurship, and Ferrazzi focuses on the important steps it takes to create, maintain, and leverage these relationships. I'm not talking about putting in a quick appearance at a professional networking cocktail hour, but actually getting to know your business associates and peers and looking for ways to help them. As entrepreneurs, we're always so busy forging new relationships with partners and clients that we tend to forget one of the most priceless opportunities out there: peer-to-peer networking. There is a wealth of knowledge within the entrepreneurial community, and a single one-on-one meeting is all it takes to realize that many of the business answers we seek could potentially come from our peers. I came to this realization some time ago and have since made it a point to proactively involve myself in the lives of fellow entrepreneurs. How do I do this? It's simple: I invite them to lunch.

I have eaten lunch with another entrepreneur, at least once per week for virtually every week for the past three years, and I have found it to be immensely rewarding on both a personal and professional level. Even the busiest executives have to eat lunch, so lunch meetings offer a way to break into someone's otherwise overbooked schedule. And a meeting over lunch offers the perfect low-pressure setting for frank discussions; in fact, in my experience, lunchtime discussions have been far more productive than a traditional business meeting would have been. Before each lunch meeting, I spend a few minutes coming up with specific questions to ask so that I can get the most out of the time we have together. I also try to think more generally about areas in which I'm seeking advice. Here are some standard questions I like to use:

- How did you start (or become involved with) your current company?

- What are your biggest challenges at the moment?

- What are some major trends in your industry?

- Are there any other people that you think I should talk to?

As you can see, these questions aren't really about me or my company—they're about the other person. Framing your questions this way implies that you are genuinely interested in hearing what they have to say, not just that you need to solve a problem and think you can get the answers out of them for the price of a cheeseburger. The last thing you want to come off as is an interrogator on a self-serving fact-finding mission. People like to talk about themselves, so asking questions about your lunch companion is an easy way to strike up a good conversation. You will likely get the answers you're looking for along the way.

By making it a habit to always have lunch with other like-minded individuals, entrepreneurs create an avenue to obtain great advice and insightful business solutions. For example, during one particularly helpful lunch, I was lamenting about my sales challenges and my inability to create an effective sales force. The entrepreneur across the table from me related how he conquered this problem in his own business. I immediately applied his lessons learned and tweaked my management approach, which led to significant revenue growth. The advice I received was simply invaluable, and all it took to get it was a few minutes over lunch.

When it comes down to it, entrepreneurs love talking to other entrepreneurs, and by tapping into these great opportunities, I come away with new insights that can help me grow my business. With so many other perspectives out there just waiting to be discovered, and five lunch hours each week to do it in, there's really no excuse to ever eat alone.

JOIN THE CLUB

Peer groups and clubs are one of the many aspects of

entrepreneurship and the startup world that took me years to appreciate. When I say peer groups, I don't mean groups designed purely for business networking. Rather, I'm talking about the kind of peer groups that function like clubs, wherein small sets of people meet regularly (monthly, if not more frequently) to discuss topics of mutual interest in an environment of trust and confidentiality. Peer-to-peer experience sharing and learning is incredibly powerful for entrepreneurs in all types of businesses, and the benefits you will reap from taking part in these kinds of groups are immeasurable.

Why are peer groups so great? They provide a safe space for you to swap stories and troubleshoot common issues with other entrepreneurs like yourself. If you have a problem you're not sure how to solve, chances are it's been tackled by someone else in your group. Not only will you learn what worked for other participants, but you'll also be able to avoid making the same mistakes they did. Conversely, if you overcame an obstacle of your own, sharing your experience with the group will probably help someone else as well.

Perhaps the biggest advantage to joining a peer group, however, is the social support you'll gain in the process. The emotional roller coaster of entrepreneurship has higher highs and lower lows than most people are used to, so it's great to have a support network of others who are going through the same things you are. No more being lonely at the top, because you're surrounded by others in similar positions. Life's a journey, and these peer groups provide a special setting in which you can develop deep and lasting relationships with other entrepreneurs.

One of the most beneficial steps I have taken as an

entrepreneur is to join the not-for-profit peer group called Entrepreneurs' Organization (EO). With chapters all over the world, EO is a global network of business owners, all of whom run companies that exceed US$1M in annual revenue. We engage leading entrepreneurs to learn and grow through executive education and other tools for business owners. There is also a similarly structured EO Accelerator program designed for entrepreneurs running companies that earn between $250K and $1M in annual revenue. In my local chapter of EO, our goal is to assemble influential entrepreneurs in the area who have a thirst for learning and peer-to-peer experience sharing. The Young Presidents' Organization (YPO) is a similar organization designed for business leaders and is active in 110 countries; it follows a similar structure and also aims to create close-knit peer groups of leaders.

A particularly valuable aspect of EO is what is known as Forum. EO Forum is a group of eight to ten entrepreneurs who meet on a regular basis, usually once a month, to participate in programs of a specific format. The Forum groups also act as each member's own personal advisory board, providing an unparalleled way to learn from other entrepreneurs how to minimize potential mistakes and maximize opportunities. By participating in a peer group that meets regularly, I've developed deeper relationships with entrepreneurs who genuinely care about each other and are there to help each other out. I'm constantly learning how other entrepreneurs run their businesses, including what works well and what doesn't.

Regardless of whether you go with a global network like EO or just a locally-based group of business owners in your own community, I wholeheartedly urge all entrepreneurs, especially first-timers, to look into joining a group of like-minded entrepreneurs with similar interests. Aside from the countless positive social aspects of belonging to such an organization, you will reap professional returns that outweigh your investment many times over.

CONSULT THE EXPERTS

I am often asked by other entrepreneurs about the merits of setting up a board of advisors. While I have employed informal advisors much more often than formal ones, I think advisors can be very valuable to a startup, and I've acted as an advisor to several companies myself. Think of advisors as ways of filling gaps or deficits in specialized expertise (e.g., product management, engineering, marketing, and so on). Another function they can fulfill involves making key introductions to customers, partners, and investors and then facilitating beneficial interactions with these players.

When recruiting advisors, look for individuals who stand out as being especially sharp or business-savvy, or people whose personal style you admire. Advisors who are also investors are ideal, as they have more skin in the game, but your board need not be composed solely or predominantly of investors. Keep in mind that getting to spend one-on-one time with the entrepreneur and with other high-quality advisors comprises a big part of the advisors' experience, so select great minds who will also get along well.

Advisors should be asked to commit for a year or two, but typically no more than that, as the needs of your startup will change over time. They should meet quarterly or bi-annually as a group over a nice dinner, in addition to meeting individually at least once between group meetings. It will be a great relief for any cash-strapped entrepreneur to learn that advisors should not be compensated with cash, but rather with equity in the company, the amount being determined by what they bring to the table (the range is typically 0.1% -1%, with the norm being closer to .25% of the startup). You might also want to offer them the opportunity to invest in each round.

While the needs of every startup are different, you'll almost always benefit from any advice dispensed by experts. I would suggest seriously considering the idea of putting together a board of advisors. You'll need to choose these advisors wisely, and you should remain present and thoroughly involved—the advisors should never act as a substitute for your input or decisions. Remember that this resource works just like any other: The more you put into it, the more you'll get out of it.

DON'T BE SHY!

Asking for help isn't a sign of weakness—it's a smart thing to do. As an entrepreneur, you'll never stop learning. And as this chapter demonstrates, there is no shortage of resources out there to assist you. Approaching a mentor is a great place to start. Don't be intimidated, and remember that the mentor will likely benefit from the arrangement as well. Also, do like I do and never eat lunch alone. Having lunch with other entrepreneurs is an easy way that you can invest just an hour each day, doing something you'd already be doing anyway, in order to get great advice and insights from others who have been where you're going. Aside from having interactions with mentors and other experienced entrepreneurs, it is important to maintain regular contact with your entrepreneurial peers. Joining an organization for novice entrepreneurs is a good way to start building relationships with others who are going through the same struggles and challenges you are.

When you're looking for answers to specific questions or quandaries, there's no better place to start than Google. There are also plenty of other web resources, such as blogs and social media outlets, that can help you solve problems and learn more about growing your business. Blogs in particular provide a never-ending source for new ideas, which will keep you informed on industry trends and recurring issues that entrepreneurs face. Subscribe to RSS feeds of your favorite blogs, and try to read as many as you can on a daily or weekly basis.

Finally, as your startup gains traction, you may want to consider putting together a board of advisors. Advisors will be chosen from successful entrepreneurs and investors in your community, and ideally they will be the "great minds" who you most admire. Their function is to provide valuable expertise to your startup, especially in areas that might otherwise be lacking. A board of advisors can really help you take your startup to the next level.

All of these avenues offer excellent opportunities to learn from others, exchange ideas and advice, keep current on industry trends, and get helpful guidance from experts. Don't be shy! You'll be surprised at how much you can benefit from the simple act of asking for help.

AFTERWORD

With regard to this guide on startups, I've admittedly launched pretty lean. Everything didn't get said. There were subjects that didn't get the attention they deserve, and important issues that didn't get addressed at all. It's a rather daunting task to attempt a complete "how to" manual on anything as complex and dynamic as entrepreneurship, but trying to write the be-all-end-all authoritative text would have meant never getting this finished book into your hands. Still, the impulse to keep thinking about these themes—to write and reflect, to dialogue with others, to ask and to question—stays with me. My next book, future blog posts, and conversations I have with entrepreneurs will be better as a direct result of feedback from readers. I am always interested in being exposed to different perspectives by hearing what others have to say about these topics.

There is no guaranteed recipe for success in startups. Every startup is different, and you'll have to find out for yourself what works and what doesn't. However, there is a pattern for success that I've seen in action many times. This approach puts corporate culture at the top of the hierarchy, with a strong foundation comprised of outstanding engineering and sales teams. Yes, all other departments—marketing, services, support, operations, and finance—are critically important to any successful company. But engineering and sales are without a doubt the most difficult variables to get right. A product doesn't have to be the best to win, but it does have to be good, so obviously engineering teams matter a great deal. And as much as tech entrepreneurs (especially those in the B2B space) would like to focus on self-service products, the reality is that people like to buy things the old-fashioned way: from other people. Therefore, sales teams also matter. Corporate culture is the overarching fabric of a company that holds everything together, and at the end of the day, it offers you and your company the only truly sustainable competitive advantage. So, if I had to compress all of my advice into a single takeaway on how to ensure your startup's success, it would read something like this: *Build a great corporate culture with strong engineering and sales and you'll be successful.*

My goal in writing this book has been not just to share my own experiences with the assumption that they'll be helpful to someone else, but also to encourage would-be entrepreneurs to take the plunge. In these challenging and uncertain economic times, more than ever before, we need to encourage the entrepreneurial spirit wherever it exists. In doing this, the hope is that more new businesses emerge, bringing with them potentially life-changing innovations as well as the jobs and monetary stimulation that our ailing economy so desperately needs. My wish is that, if I accomplished nothing else with this exercise, I've at least succeeded in convincing a brave few to believe in their dreams and to keep working to make them happen.

50 Tips for Entrepreneurs

Here are 50 things every startup entrepreneur should know, in no particular order.

1. Just do it!
2. 99% of all decisions aren't permanent.
3. Be slow to hire and quick to fire.
4. Measure what you manage.
5. Competition isn't as important as the customer.
6. 95% of startups shouldn't raise money.
7. Join a startup peer group.
8. The biggest challenge with growth is keeping everyone aligned.
9. Price isn't a sustainable differentiator; customer service is.
10. Market timing is the most important factor for hitting a startup homerun.
11. Empower current customers to help win over and recruit new customers.
12. Create the best possible working environment for your team.
13. Asking good questions is more important than guessing the right answers.
14. Build relationships before you need them.

15. Always consider the best alternative outcome before beginning a negotiation.

16. Consciously balance time working *in* the business vs. time working *on* the business.

17. You only get one first impression.

18. What you start out doing isn't likely where you'll find your greatest success.

19. Get your corporate culture right and everything will fall into place.

20. The best exit strategy is not to need one.

21. A website's biggest enemy is the browser *Back* button.

22. Recurring revenue is the best form of revenue.

23. Don't burn any bridges—it's a small world.

24. Build a niche brand and curate all aspects of it.

25. Pivoting and iterating is healthy and necessary in a startup.

26. Always ask for a discount.

27. Your idea isn't unique. But the way you execute it is.

28. Sharing your idea with others will lead to benefits you can't predict.

29. Keep it as simple as possible.

30. People identify with companies or brands more so than specific products.

31. It's usually worth paying a professional to do things right the first time.

32. Set goals and adapt to changing information.

33. Storytelling is more powerful than marketing.

34. Most startups initially price their product or service too low.

35. Make time to think and reflect.

36. Focus on rhythm, data, and priorities, and the rest will take care of itself.

37. Develop offline analogies to describe your startup.

38. Companies aren't just about profits.

39. Celebrate the small victories.

40. Play to your strengths.

41. Be opinionated about your product when considering customer suggestions.

42. Know why you're different and articulate it clearly.

43. Don't develop products in a vacuum.

44. Regularly communicate with employees, customers, investors, and the community.

45. Remove friction for all stakeholders.

46. Transparency is important because, absent information, people make stuff up.

47. It is difficult to concentrate on more than three things at any one time.

48. Employees are the most important stakeholder.

49. No plan is perfect. Think of revisions as improvements.

50. Consume the startup—don't let it consume you.

RECOMMENDED BLOGS

I subscribe to a number of blogs and online periodicals via Google Reader. This is a great way for me to keep up to date on news and trends without spending half my day clicking around to a bunch of bookmarked sites. Instead, I just scan the newest feed items each day, stopping to read the ones that interest me most in their entirety. Naturally, I'm biased towards technology and startup blogs, but I try to include as diverse a selection as possible. Here's a shortened list of the blogs I subscribe to at the moment:

- A VC
- Above the Crowd
- B2B Lead Generation Blog
- B2B Marketing ROI
- B2B Sales Pipeline
- Blog Maverick
- Both Sides of the Table
- Build A Sales Machine
- cdixon.org
- Coding Horror
- Customer Experience Matrix

- For Entrepreneurs
- Force of Good
- Get Venture
- GigaOM
- Hacker News
- Infectious Greed
- infoChachkie
- Joel on Software
- Kellblog
- Kottke
- Lessons Learned
- Marc Andreessen
- MarketingAutomation.net
- Musings of an Entrepreneur
- PaulStamatiou.com
- ReadWriteWeb
- Redeye VC
- TechCrunch

RECOMMENDED BOOKS

Agassi, Andre. *Open: An Autobiography*. New York: AKA Publishing, LLC, 2009.

Berry, Tim. *The Plan-as-You-Go Business Plan*. Eliot, ME: Eliot House Productions, 2008.

Bogle, John. *Enough: True Measures of Money, Business, and Life*. Hoboken, NJ: John Wiley & Sons, Inc., 2009.

Branson, Richard. *Business Stripped Bare: Adventures of a Global Entrepreneur*. New York: Random House, 2009.

-----. *Losing My Virginity: How I've Survived, Had Fun, and Made a Fortune Doing Business My Way*. New York: Crown Business, 2010.

Burlingham, Bo. *Small Giants: Companies that Choose to be Great Instead of Big*. New York:Penguin Group, 2005.

Catlin, Katherine, & Jana Matthews. *Learning at the Speed of Growth*. New York: Hungry Minds, 2001.

Collins, James & William C. Lazier. *Beyond Entrepreneurship: Turning Your Business into an Enduring Great Company*. New York: Prentice Hall, 1992.

Cummings, David, & Adam Blitzer. *Think Outside the Inbox: The B2B Marketing Automation Guide*. Atlanta: Leigh Walker, 2009.

Drucker, Peter F. *The Daily Drucker*. Oxford, UK: Linacre House, 2005.

Ferrazzi, Keith. *Who's Got Your Back: The Breakthrough Program to Build Deep Trusting Relationships that Create Success—and Won't Let You Fail.* New York: Crown Publishing, 2009.

Ferrazzi, Keith & Tahl Raz. *Never Eat Alone: And Other Secrets to Success, One Relationship at a Time.* New York: Crown Business, 2005.

Fried, Jason, David Hansson Heinemeier, & Matthew Linderman, eds. *Getting Real: The Smarter, Faster, Easier Way to Build a Successful Web Application.* Chicago: 37signals, 2009.

Gladwell, Malcolm. *Outliers: The Story of Success*. New York: Little, Brown & Co., 2008.

Goldratt, Elivahu M., & Jeff Cox. *The Goal: A Process of Ongoing Improvement.* Gower Publishing, 2004.

Harnish, Verne. *Mastering the Rockefeller Habits: What You Must Do to Increase the Value of Your Fast Growing Firm.* New York: Select Books, 2002.

Heath, Chip, & Dan Heath. *Switch: How to Change Things When Change is Hard.* New York: Broadway Books, 2010.

Hickerson, Craig, Tom Smith, & Roger Connors. *The Oz Principle: Getting Results through Individual and Organizational Accountability.* New York: Prentice Hall, 1994.

Kaplan, Jerry. *Startup: A Silicon Valley Adventure.* New York: Penguin, 1994

Konrath, Jill. *Selling to Big Companies*. New York: Dearborn Trade Publishing, 2006.

-----. *SNAP Selling: Speed Up Sales and Win More Business With Today's Frazzled Customers*. New York: Penguin Group, 2010.

Kram, Kathy E. *Mentoring at Work: Developmental Relationships in Organizational Life*. Boston: University Press of America, 1988.

Lencioni, Patrick. *The Five Dysfunctions of a Team*. San Francisco: Jossey-Bass, 2002.

-----. *The Five Temptations of a CEO*. San Francisco: Jossey-Bass, 1998.

-----. *Silos, Politics, and Turf Wars*. San Francisco: Jossey-Bass, 1996.

Lewis, Michael. *Liar's Poker: Rising Through the Wreckage on Wall Street*. New York: W. W. Norton, 2010.

-----. *Moneyball: The Art of Winning an Unfair Game*. New York: W. W. Norton, 2004.

Levinson, Jay Conrad (Ed.). *The Ultimate Sales Machine: Turbocharge Your Business With Relentless Focus on 12 Key Strategies*. New York: Penguin Group, 2007.

Livingston, Jessica. *Founders at Work: Stories of Startups' Early Days*. Berkeley, CA: Apress, 2008.

Pink, Daniel. *Drive: The Surprising Truth About What Motivates Us*. New

York: Penguin Group, 2009.

Perkins, Tom. *Valley Boy: The Education of Tom Perkins.* New York: Gotham, 2008.

Prosen, Bob. *Kiss Theory Good Bye: Five Proven Ways to Get Extraordinary Results in Any Company.* Dallas, TX: Goldpen Publishing, 2006.

Robbins, Anthony. *Awaken the Giant Within: How to Take Immediate Control of Your Mental, Emotional, Physical and Financial Destiny.* New York: Freepress, 1991.

Smart, Bradford D. *Topgrading: How Leading Companies Win By Hiring, Coaching and Keeping the Best People.* New York: Penguin, 2005.

Smart, Bradford D., & Greg Alexander. *Topgrading for Sales: World-Class Methods to Interview, Hire and Coach Top Sales Representatives.* New York: Penguin, 2008.

Southon, Mike, & Chris West. *The Beermat Entrepreneur: Turn Your Good Idea Into a Great Business.* Financial Times Management, 2002.

Stack, Jack, & Bo Burlingham. *The Great Game of Business.* New York: Doubleday, 1992.

Taleb, Nassim Nicholas. *The Black Swan: The Impact of the Highly Improbable.* New York: Random House, 2010.

Turner, Ted, & Bill Burke. *Call Me Ted.* New York: Grand Central Publishing, 2008.

ABOUT THE AUTHOR

David Cummings has been an entrepreneur and business and technology enthusiast for over ten years. In 2001 he founded Hannon Hill Corporation, now an Inc. 500 company and a leading provider of web content management solutions for the higher education and government industry verticals. He has since started four more companies: Pardot, a marketing automation SaaS provider; Clickscape, a technology-driven real estate agency; Rigor, a web performance toolset; and SalesLoft, makers of sales intelligence software. Pardot was named the fastest growing technology company in Atlanta in 2010 by the Atlanta Business Chronicle.

David has lectured on startups and technology at Duke University, Emory University, and the Georgia Institute of Technology. He has also presented at the Silicon Valley Web Guild, Advanced Technology Development Center, and the Technology Association of Georgia. He serves on the board of the Atlanta chapter of Entrepreneurs' Organization and on the board of Venture Atlanta. A native of Tallahassee, Florida, David earned a Bachelor of Science degree in economics from Duke University and studied at the London School of Economics. David co-authored his first book, *Think Outside the Inbox: The B2B Marketing Automation Guide*, with Pardot COO Adam Blitzer.

NOTES

Introduction

[1] U.S. Small Business Administration data.
http://www.sba.gov/advocacy/7495/8425
[2] SCORE, "Small Biz Stats & Trends."
http://www.score.org/node/148155
[3] Ewing Marion Kaufman Foundation. "Despite Recession, U.S. Entrepreneurial Activity Rises in 2009 to Highest Rate in 14 Years, Kauffman Study Shows," *Kaufman Index of Entrepreneurial Activity,* 20 May 2010. http://www.kauffman.org/newsroom/despite-recession-us-entrepreneurial-activity-rate-rises-in-2009.aspx
[4] U.S. Small Business Administration, "Frequently Asked Questions." http://www.sba.gov/advocacy/7495

Chapter 1

[5] Bill Rancic, quoted in "Quotations about Famous Entrepreneurs on Entrepreneurship."
http://entrepreneurs.about.com/od/famousentrepreneurs/a/quotations.htm
[6] Kaufman Foundation, Ibid.
[7] FedEx corporate website, "FedEx History."
http://about.fedex.designcdt.com/our_company/company_information/fedex_history
[8] Nate Jackson, "Survey released of top ten retailers for customer service," *LA Times* blog, 23 November 2010.
http://latimesblogs.latimes.com/money_co/2010/11/nrf-releases-survey-of-top-ten-retailers-for-customer-service.html

[9] Tara Hunt, "Power to Change the Broken System," *Horsepigcow* blog (*PNT: Gazette Edition)*, 2 January 2010.
http://www.horsepigcow.com/?s=monetization

[10] Tim Berry, "Heart of a Business: Market, Identity and Focus," *Planning Startups Stories* blog (on Bplans website), 11 October 2007.
http://timberry.bplans.com/2007/10/heart-of-a-bu-1.html#ixzz16bzfJjeW

[11] Mark Suster, "Domain Experience Gives Entrepreneurs an Unfair Advantage," *Both Sides of the Table* blog, 7 February 2010.
http://www.bothsidesofthetable.com/2010/02/07/domain-experience-gives-entrepreneurs-an-unfair-advantage

Chapter 3

[12] Bill Gates, "Shaping the Internet Age," *Internet Policy Institute*, December 2000.
http://www.microsoft.com/presspass/exec/billg/writing/shapingtheinternet.mspx

[13] Pew Research Center, "The Future of the Internet IV," research series for *Internet and American Life Project*, 19 February 2010.
http://www.pewinternet.org/Reports/2010/Future-of-the-Internet-IV.aspx

[14] Jens Lapinski, "List of VC Funds," *Founder's View* blog, 14 April 2009. http://jenslapinski.wordpress.com/2009/04/14/list-of-vc-funds

[15] "A Grim Year for Small Business Lending," *CNN Money*, 1 October 2009.
http://money.cnn.com/2009/10/01/smallbusiness/sba_annual_lending_overview/index.htm

[16] Quoted in Jay Rizoli, "Friends and family financing remains at the heart of most startups," *Mass High Tech*, 31 October 2008.
http://www.masshightech.com/stories/2008/10/27/focus5-Friends-and-family-financing-remains-at-the-heart-of-most-startups.html

Chapter 4

[17] Google official website,"Google history."
http://www.google.com/about/corporate/company/history.html

[18] Cited in Erick Scholfeld, "Peter Thiel: 'Best Predictor of Startup Success is Low CEO Pay'," *TechCrunch*, 8 September 2008.
http://techcrunch.com/2008/09/08/peter-thiel-best-predictor-of-startup-success-is-low-ceo-pay

[19] Mike Southon and Chris West, *The Beermat Entrepreneur: Turn Your Good Idea Into a Great Business.* 2nd Edition. New York: Pearson Prentice Hall, 2005.

[20] Patrick Lencioni, *Death by Meeting: A Leadership Fable...About Solving the Most Painful Problem in Business.* (Jossey-Bass, 2004)

[21] Chris Morrison, "The Perfect Startup Team? Grey Hair and Mohawks," *Venture Beat*, 26 March 2010.
http://entrepreneur.venturebeat.com/2010/03/26/the-perfect-startup-team-grey-hair-and-mohawks

[22] Sean Wise, "The Talent Triangle," *The Globe and Mail*, 17 May 2006 [updated 5 April 2009]. http://www.theglobeandmail.com/report-on-business/article826049.ece

[23] Bradford D Smart, *Topgrading: How Leading Companies Win By Hiring, Coaching, and Keeping the Best People.* New York: Penguin, 2005.

[24] Small Business Notes, "Interviewing Guidelines."
http://www.smallbusinessnotes.com/operating/hr/hiring/interviewing.html

Chapter 5

[25] Dale Willerton, "A Good Business in a Bad Location Will Be a Bad Business," *Blue MauMau*, 24 February 2010.
http://www.bluemaumau.org/successful_site_selection_good_business_poor_location_will_become_poor_business

[26] "SBE Council Releases Small Business Survival Index 2009," *Small*

Business Trends, 6 December 2009.
http://smallbiztrends.com/2009/12/sbe-council-releases-index-2009-ranking-the-states.html

[27] Kurt Badenhausen, "The Best States for Business," *Forbes*, 23 September 2009. http://www.forbes.com/2009/09/23/best-states-for-business-beltway-best-states.html

[28] Jennifer Lawinski, "Eight Cities That Want Your Business," *CNN Money*, 23 November 2010.
http://money.cnn.com/galleries/2010/smallbusiness/1011/gallery.cities_to_start_a_small_business.smb/index.html

Chapter 6

[29] Kail Padgitt, "2011 State Business Tax Climate Index" (8th Edition), *Tax Foundation*, 26 October 2010.
http://www.taxfoundation.org/research/show/22658.html

[30] Hewlett-Packard official website, "HP Garage" brief.
http://www8.hp.com/us/en/pdf/brief_tcm_245_948414.pdf

[31] Cicorp company website, "Steve Jobs' [*sic*] Garage."
http://cicorp.com/Apple/garage/index.htm

[32] "Google's Garage: Home Sweet Home," *WIRED*, 1 October 2006.
http://www.wired.com/techbiz/media/news/2006/10/71888

[33] Marty Neumeier, *Zag*. (Berkeley, CA: New Riders, 2007) p.53

Chapter 7

[34] Ernst Malmsten, *Boo Hoo: A dot.com Story from Concept to Catastrophe*. (New York: Random House Business Books, 2001).

Chapter 8

[35] "The lean startup," *Lessons Learned* blog, 8 September 2008. [Emphasis added.]

http://www.startuplessonslearned.com/2008/09/lean-startup.html

[36] Eric Ries, "The three drivers of growth for your business mode. Choose one," *Lessons Learned* blog, 22 September 2008. http://www.startuplessonslearned.com/2008/09/three-drivers-of-growth-for-your.html

[37] Rosabeth Moss Kanter, "Find the 15 Minute Competitive Advantage," *Harvard Business Review*, 9 November 2009. http://blogs.hbr.org/kanter/2009/11/find-the-15minute-competitive.html

Chapter 9

[38] Bradford D. Smart and Greg Alexander, *Topgrading for Sales.* (New York: Portfolio, 2008).

[39] Mark Suster, "Startup Sales – Why Hiring Seasoned Sales Reps May Not Work," *Both Sides of the Table* blog, 12 October 2010. http://www.bothsidesofthetable.com/2010/10/12/startup-sales-why-hiring-seasoned-reps-may-not-work

[40] Tam Harbert, "How Much Should You Expect to Pay a Recruiter?" *AllBusiness.* http://www.allbusiness.com/labor-employment/human-resources-personnel-management/7606468-1.html

[41] Darmesh Shah, "Building Startup Sales Teams: Tips for Founders," *OnStartups* blog, 3 August 2009. http://onstartups.com/tabid/3339/bid/10155/Building-Startup-Sales-Teams-Tips-For-Founders.aspx

Chapter 10

[42] Adam Blitzer, "Social Networking: How B2B Companies Can Leverage This Trend," *B2B Marketing ROI* blog, 27 May 2008. http://b2bmarketingroi.com/2008/05/27/social-networking-how-b2b-companies-can-leverage-this-trend

[43] Michael Greene, "B2B Interactive Spending Will Double by 2014," *Forrester Research*, 4 March 2010.

http://forrester.com/rb/Research/b2b_interactive_spend_will_double_by
_2014/q/id/56417/t/2

[44] Facebook official website, "Statistics."
http://www.facebook.com/press/info.php?statistics

[45] Adam Blitzer, "Social Networking."

[46] Beth Negus Viveiros, "More Marketers Using Email for Prospecting: Survey," *Chief Marketer*, 12 April 2011.
http://chiefmarketer.com/research/cm-prospecting-survey-2011

[47] For more detailed information, download the whole whitepaper, *Four T's of Effective Email Campaigns*, at
http://www.pardot.com/company/white-papers/effective-email.html.

Chapter 11

[48] Tim Berry, "10 Tips for Saving Your Life From Your Business," *Planning Startups Stories* blog, 15 December 2009.
http://timberry.bplans.com/2009/12/10-tips-for-saving-your-life-from-your-business.html

[49] Zappos official website, "Zappos Family Core Values."
http://about.zappos.com/our-unique-culture/zappos-core-values

[50] Kathy Kram, *Mentoring at Work: Developmental Relationships in Organizational Life.* (Lanham, MD: University Press of America, 1988).

Chapter 12

[51] Case study by Prof. Noam Wasserman, cited in Julia Hanna, "Surviving Success: When Founders Must Go," *Working Knowledge* (Harvard Business School), 4 October 2006.
http://hbswk.hbs.edu/item/5480.html

[52] Lance Weatherby, "Startups: The Growth Stage," *Force of Good* blog, 21 July 2009. http://blog.weatherby.net/2009/07/startups-the-growth-stage.html

[53] Ibid.

Chapter 13

[54] Tim Berry, "10 Tips for Saving Your Life From Your Business."

Chapter 14

[55] Kathy Kram, *Mentoring at Work.*
[56] Ibid.

11731951R00177

Made in the USA
Charleston, SC
17 March 2012